AT LAST!

The KANSAS CITY CHIEFS' Unforgettable 2019 Championship Season

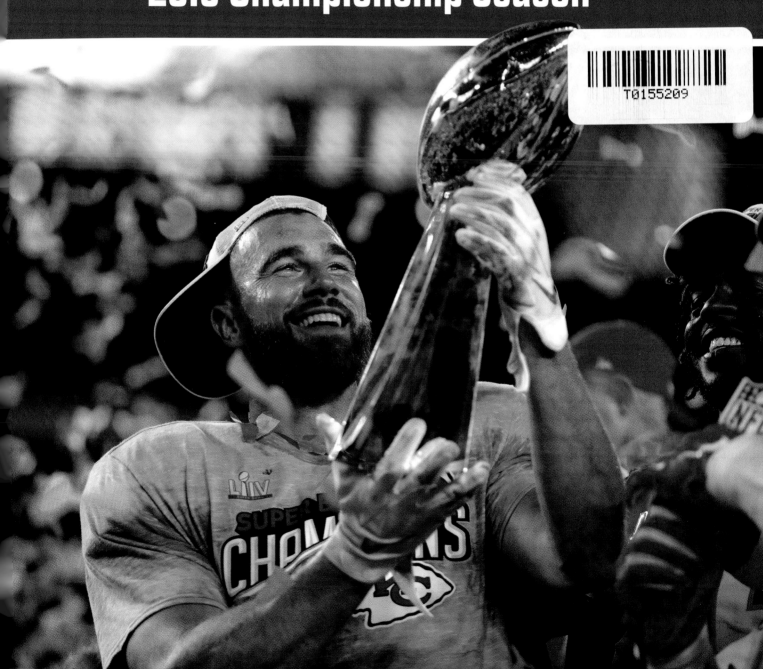

Chiefs players douse head coach Andy Reid with gatorade as the clock runs down in the fourth quarter.

This book is available in quantity at special discounts for your group or organization.
For further information, contact:

Triumph Books LLC
814 North Franklin Street
Chicago, Illinois 60610
Phone: (312) 337-0747
www.triumphbooks.com

Printed in U.S.A.
ISBN: 978-1-62937-710-0

Content packaged by Mojo Media, Inc.
Joe Funk: Editor
Jason Hinman: Creative Director

Front and back cover photos by AP Images

All interior photos by AP Images

CONTENTS

Foreword

By Kevin Harlan

There are so many ways to view the Kansas City Chiefs winning their first Super Bowl title in 50 years.

Through the eyes of the players who – some old, some new – perhaps learned a lot from last season's gut-wrenching finish.

Through the eyes of head coach Andy Reid who has built a winner again, as he had previously in Philadelphia, making it back to a Super Bowl, as he did with the Eagles, but this timing finally claiming the coveted Vince Lombardi Trophy.

Most poignantly, through the eyes of the Hunt family. Founder Lamar Hunt's son, Clark, now runs the team and accepted the AFC Championship trophy bearing his father's name. The late Lamar Hunt's wife Norma, holding, then kissing the trophy in maybe the most poignant moment of all.

How do you describe the kind of elation and pure joy of being at Arrowhead when the Chiefs captured the AFC Championship? In the stands as the clock wound down and it was apparent the Chiefs would indeed win, the crowd almost didn't know how to react. This was new territory. The Chiefs had been so close last season and it was grabbed away at the last moment by a Hall of Fame quarterback and coach of the most successful NFL team of the last two decades, who knew how to close the deal. The Patriots had been there. They knew the course well. They knew how.

For the Chiefs, and their fans, well, they hadn't been down that road. So again, disappointment. Crushing disappointment. That's the road they knew. They had been there. That was a course they knew well.

Finally, zeros on the clock. It was finished. As the benches emptied and the game ended, I took my binoculars and looked down from our high broadcast position at Arrowhead, not to look at the players on the field celebrating, but rather I looked to the stands below. And there I saw grown men and women crying and hugging anyone within reach.

Winning the Super Bowl takes those emotions to a whole different level. I mean it had been 50 years, a lifetime, since the Chiefs had been to a Super Bowl. And to be so close a year ago and lose the way they did, man, that was a tough one to process. For the team and fans.

Watching the Chiefs seal the win in Super Bowl LIV was especially unique for fans who were lucky enough to be around for Super Bowl IV, the last time the Chiefs were crowned champions. Of course, every Chiefs fan was ecstatic after the Super Bowl LIV win, but these veteran fans had been through a lot in 50 years. It's like seeing a long-lost friend, college or high school buddy, or relative you hadn't seen in forever. Someone who had been such an important part of your life, a lifetime ago, who you hadn't seen in decades. That kind of reunion, that kind of emotional sequence, is extremely hard to describe. The emotions that come out of that reunion are very raw and real. You can't disguise that feeling.

So that's why, because it was so unrehearsed and genuine, so organic to the moment, it was fascinating to watch. No pretense. No macho. No hiding emotion.

Andy Reid and Patrick Mahomes are all smiles during their post-game interview in Miami.

There was nothing to hide behind or cover your true feelings. So revealing. Very impactful. There was nothing to say, really. It spoke for itself with thousands and thousands of Chiefs fans sharing a very unique moment. That is what I will remember. Strangers. Family. Chiefs fans. Pure joy.

For most Chiefs fans that have waited season after season and known the heartbreak of losing, or coming close, or not even being a factor over the last 50 seasons, I wonder if their joy would be as full if they hadn't endured all that had happened. All those seasons of hope. All those losing seasons. And everything in between. They probably have more appreciation for this trip to the Super Bowl than most NFL fans. The only fans that could relate are fans of teams that have never been there. But 50 years? Come on. That's a lifetime.

In life, they say the journey is the reward. Well, Chiefs fans have been rewarded for their incredible patience and loyalty on a journey few fan bases have had to endure. Yet, they still came to Arrowhead. Still bought tickets. Tailgated. Cheered. What loyalty! And that I think makes them the best fans in the NFL. ∎

Introduction

When the Kansas City Chiefs became world champions of football with the upset triumph over the Minnesota Vikings in Super Bowl IV, it seemed the beginning of a new era rather than the ending of another.

The 1969 season marked the end of 10-year run of the American Football League, the upstart brainchild of Chiefs founder Lamar Hunt. The Chiefs franchise dominated the decade, winning three AFL championships and playing in Super Bowl I before winning the final AFL-NFL title game before the two leagues merged. The Chiefs were a model franchise poised for the future with 10 future members of the Pro Football Hall of Fame within the organization.

The only things that followed, however, were disappointments and sadness. For 50 years the Chiefs wandered the NFL desert searching for an oasis. The painful losses started on Christmas Day 1971, when the Chiefs fell 27-24 to the Miami Dolphins in double overtime, the longest game in NFL history.

The Chiefs would only make the playoffs twice in the next 19 seasons and it would be a full 20 years before they won a playoff game. For 50 seasons Chiefs fans would continue to support the kingdom despite countless disappointments and heartbreaks.

The 2019 season started with more optimism than any campaign in Chiefs history. Coming four inches short of the Super Bowl, as Andy Reid preached all offseason, left this team hungry but also expectant. Another trip to the AFC Championship game wasn't the goal but a step along the way.

But nothing worth having comes without sacrifice and challenges. The 2019 Chiefs faced their share of stops and starts, with times where a Super Bowl didn't seem in the cards this season.

There was no lower point for the Chiefs than the sight of quarterback Patrick Mahomes down on the field in Denver. There wasn't a Chiefs fan who didn't feel sick to their stomach seeing the MVP on the turf with a team physician repositioning his dislocated right kneecap back into place.

The near miraculous return of Mahomes to the field ushered in a resurgence of the Chiefs' Super Bowl hopes, but it took more than that to return a franchise to a glory it hadn't experienced for five decades.

Last March Chiefs general manager Brett Veach went on the free agent market looking for a new defensive leader. The team already had in Mahomes a leader on offense. Now the team need a quarterback on defense.

From the moment Tyrann Mathieu arrived in Kansas City, he preached the need for "championship swagger." Veach also added defensive end Frank Clark via a trade with Seattle, bringing Mathieu a partner in crime in reinvigorating a dormant defense.

Mahomes returned to the lineup in Week 10, but a disheartening loss to the Tennessee Titans left the Chiefs sitting at 6-4, losers of four of their last six games. This no longer seemed the dream season the Chiefs and their fans envisioned.

But a funny thing happened on the way to the offseason. The Chiefs started winning. The defense got better. Then it got a lot better. The once-unstoppable offense became unstoppable again.

For 50 years the Chiefs' path to a Super Bowl was littered with roadblocks. Now the path cleared before them. A miraculous confluence of events in Week 17 led to the Chiefs earning the No. 2 seed and a first-round bye.

That edge came in handy when the Chiefs fell behind

Andy Reid celebrates on the field with his wife, Tammy, and tight end Travis Kelce.

the Houston Texans in the Divisional Playoff round and needed some Arrowhead Stadium magic for a stunning come-from-behind victory. Then, instead of visiting the Baltimore Ravens and league MVP Lamar Jackson, the Chiefs hosted the No. 6 seed Tennessee Titans in the AFC Championship game.

That's not usually how it goes for the Chiefs. But maybe it does now. Kansas City's fortunes started to change. First came Reid, whose arrival in 2013 brought a new culture and a breath of fresh air to an organization in need of healing.

And then came Mahomes. The Chiefs have never truly had a quarterback to call their own. Pro Football Hall of Fame quarterback Len Dawson came to the Chiefs from the senior NFL. The Chiefs tried castoffs

and hand me downs, but the Joe Montanas and the Alex Smiths of the football world couldn't get the Chiefs to the promised land.

The last 20 years of the NFL has been dominated by the names Brady, Manning, Roethlisberger, Brees and Rodgers. Now Mahomes leads the list of quarterbacks opening a new era in the NFL.

Future generations of Chiefs fans will never understand the trials and tribulations faced by their predecessors. The Super Bowl LIV triumph by Mahomes and the Chiefs closes the door on a half century of disappointment. The franchise now embarks on a journey toward a new golden age led by an NFL MVP, emboldened by a Vince Lombardi Trophy and driven to make the next 50 years different. ■

Super Bowl LIV

Chiefs 31, 49ers 20
February 2, 2020 • Miami Gardens, Florida

Miracle in Miami

Comeback Kids Make It Three-Straight Wins Rallying from Double-Digit Deficits, Bring a Championship Back to Kansas City

With just under nine minutes left in the fourth quarter of Super Bowl LIV, the Chiefs offense took the field trailing the San Francisco 49ers 20-10. Their previous two drives ended with interceptions, and none of the usual Patrick Mahomes magic could be found inside Hard Rock Stadium.

Just when you count Mahomes and the Chiefs out, however, is exactly when they find the will to win.

"I think any time you have a guy like Pat Mahomes and all of the skill guys we have on offense, you never should have a reason to flinch," said safety Tyrann Mathieu.

The Chiefs didn't flinch, and Mahomes engineered three-straight fourth-quarter touchdown drives, each one faster than the last, in lifting Kansas City to a 31-20 triumph, securing the club's first Super Bowl championship in 50 years.

The Chiefs took some time settling in, going three-and-out on their first drive. The 49ers used a 32-yard run on a reverse to receiver Deebo Samuel to advance into Kansas City territory, but the Chiefs defense held the 49ers to a 38-yard field from Robbie Gould.

The Chiefs started to get rolling offensively on their second drive, embarking on a methodical 15-play, 75-yard drive draining more than seven minutes off the clock. Mahomes finished the drive with a 1-yard touchdown on an option run to put Kansas City on the board.

The first mistake of the game belonged to San Francisco quarterback Jimmy Garoppolo. On the second play of the second quarter, he tried to throw the ball away while facing pressure on a second-and-12. The ball didn't get out of bounds, however, and cornerback Bashaud Breeland picked off the errant throw.

"That defense played their tails off," said tight end Travis Kelce. "When we needed stops, they won us the game."

Nine plays after the interception, kicker Harrison Butker hit a field goal from 31 yards out and put the Chiefs up 10-3.

The 49ers responded quickly, however, driving 80 yards in seven plays. Garoppolo connected with fullback Kyle Juszczyk for a 15-yard touchdown to tie the game.

The 10-10 score at halftime stood as a rarity – it was just the fourth time in Super Bowl history the game headed into halftime with a tied score.

Coming out of the long halftime break, the 49ers assumed command early. San Francisco received the opening kick of the second half and went 60 yards in nine to plays before settling for a Gould field goal from 42 yards put them up 13-10.

Mahomes struggled again opening the second half, throwing interceptions on each of the team's first two second-half possessions.

Patrick Mahomes rolls out against the 49ers during the Chiefs' second-half comeback effort.

Defensive end Frank Clark said the team never had doubts despite the early struggles.

"When you're a defender and you've got an offense who you trust in, and you're an offense and you've got a defense who you trust in, things like that happen," Clark said. "Special things happen. Tonight, that outcome is something magical happened."

The Chiefs needed a quick score, and Mahomes got the job done. Thanks to a big third-and-15 conversion with a 44-yard completion to Tyreek Hill, Mahomes moved Kansas City 83 yards in 2 minutes, 40 seconds. The quarterback capped off the drive with a 1-yard touchdown pass to Kelce.

After the defense stopped the 49ers three-and-out, Mahomes drove this Chiefs 65 yards in just 2:26. This time, running back Damien Williams took it into the end zone from five yards out for the score. Williams appeared close to stepping out of bounds before

Opposite: Patrick Mahomes celebrates running for the Chiefs' first touchdown of the night. Above: Defensive end Frank Clark makes a key fourth down tackle during the fourth quarter. It was the Chiefs' first sack of the night.

breaking into the end zone, but an official review upheld the call on the field.

After that, the Chiefs defense continued shutting down the 49ers and got the ball back with a chance to ice the game. The Chiefs simply needed a first down to run out the clock, but Williams cut through a demoralized 49ers defense for a 38-yard touchdown run that extended the lead.

The fourth-quarter defensive stops were something the Chiefs couldn't get a year ago when they fell to the New England Patriots in overtime of the AFC Championship game. This time, however, the rebuilt defense under coordinator Steve Spagnuolo made the plays it needed. That's what makes this team a champion, said defensive end Chris Jones.

"When the defense is playing lights out, defense steps up and makes a stop, that's all Pat needs," Jones said. "He's going to make something happen, the receiving corps going to make something happen. We put them in a position to make plays and guess what? They excelled."

Opposite: Running back Damien Williams crosses the goal line for a fourth quarter touchdown that gave the Chiefs the lead. Above: Cornerback Charvarius Ward moves to take down 49ers wide receiver Kendrick Bourne during the second half.

The victory ended two historic Super Bowl droughts. Reid finally broke through with the first title in his 21-year coaching career, and the family of Lamar Hunt finally returned the Lombardi Trophy to one of the league's most respected franchises.

"I'm happy for the Hunt family most of all," Reid said. "They've been through a lot over the years. For them to have this back in their hands, I think is tremendous. And for the city of Kansas City, it's great."

Mahomes said he had two goals when he became the starting quarterback for the Chiefs. One was to bring the Lamar Hunt Trophy awarded to the AFC champion to Kansas City. The second was getting Reid a Super Bowl ring.

"He's one of the greatest coaches of all time," Mahomes said. "I don't think he needed the Lombardi Trophy to prove that. But just to do that, it puts all doubt aside, and he's going to be listed as one of the all-time great coaches in history whenever he wants to be done, which I hope is not anytime soon."

Yes, the Chiefs are already thinking of winning this thing again. ■

The Chiefs defense put on the pressure late, when it was needed most. Above: Damien Williams celebrates his second touchdown of the game.

Terry Bradshaw congratulates Kansas City Chiefs owner Clark Hunt and Norma Hunt during the trophy presentation.

'Pat Being Pat'

Mahomes Finds More Magic in MVP Performance

For the better part of three and half quarters in Super Bowl LIV, Patrick Mahomes didn't look anything like a most valuable player.

When he walked onto the field with 8:53 remaining in the game, Mahomes had completed 18-of-29 passing for 172 yards and two interceptions with his team trailing by 10.

"I just tried to fight, and obviously the third quarter didn't go the way I wanted it to," Mahomes said. "I tried to force some things and had some turnovers."

Those final 8 minutes and 53 seconds showed exactly why Mahomes is the new face of not just the Chiefs but the NFL. The 24-year-old wunderkind finished the game sizzling, completing 8-of-13 passing for 114 yards and two scores in rallying his team to a 31-20 victory over San Francisco.

"Showtime Mahomes is going to find whoever he needs to find to get us down the field," said tight end Travis Kelce.

Despite the 10-point deficit, Mahomes patrolled the sidelines telling his team to have faith and believe that a rally would come, wide receiver Tyreek Hill said.

"He brought the guys together, and you saw what happened," Hill said. "We pulled it off."

Mahomes even delivered another of his trademark breathtaking plays that turned the momentum in his team's favor. Facing a third-and-15 with just over seven minutes remaining, Mahomes drifted back to his left until wide receiver Tyreek Hill slipped past the 49ers' secondary, hauling in a 44-yard bomb.

"We were in a bad situation, especially with that pass rush," Mahomes said. "You knew those guys had their ears pinned back and they were going to be rushing. I think the offensive line gave me enough time to throw a really deep route, and I just put it out there and Tyreek made a really great play and so that got us going there. We were able to get it down there and score that drive and then got the ball back because the defense got a nice stop."

Wide receiver Sammy Watkins called Mahomes "the golden child."

"When you have one of the best quarterbacks in the league, my job is easy," Watkins said. "My job is to go out there and be in the right place and let Pat do what he does. He's one of the best quarterbacks in my eyes."

Head coach Andy Reid said Mahomes kept firing despite the early miscues.

"The guys around him just believed in him," Reid said. "We all did, all the coaches likewise."

The comeback underscored why teammate Frank Clark believes the Chiefs can rally from any situation, no matter how dire the circumstances.

"You know Pat Mahomes," Clark said. "Like I've been saying all year, I'll take that quarterback over any quarterback. There's none like him."

The poise under pressure that Mahomes put on display is what offensive coordinator Eric Bieniemy said he sees every day.

"He's a come early, stay late guy," Bieniemy said. "He strives for perfection in order to achieve excellence. That's just who he is."

Seven years ago, Mahomes mused on Twitter how amazing it would feel to "be the quarterback who says, 'I'm going to Disney World' after winning the Super Bowl." Now, that's him.

"You dream about this stuff when you're a little kid," Mahomes said. "I just try to go out there and be the best person I can be every single day, and I enjoy this every single day. I enjoy going to the facility. I enjoy watching film. I enjoy most of all the brotherhood a team builds." ■

Patrick Mahomes and teammates are presented with the Vince Lombardi trophy.

Championship Template

Seven Years of Moves Help Chiefs Build Super Bowl Team

Kansas City's path to a championship started at the very bottom. The 2012 Chiefs finished with a 2-14 record, the worst performance in franchise history. Jamaal Charles somehow managed to rush for 1,509 yards that season, but otherwise the Chiefs endured nothing but frustration, futility and tragedy.

On Dec. 31, 2012, team chairman and CEO Clark Hunt dismissed head coach Romeo Crennel and four days later terminated general manager Scott Pioli. Hunt made a decision to break with tradition in hiring a new general manager who would in turn hire a head coach. He wanted both positions to report to him, starting with a "proven leader" as a head coach. That decision set the Chiefs' bid for a championship in motion.

January 4, 2013: Hiring Andy Reid

Hunt moved swiftly to fill the vacant head coaching position, tabbing Reid as the team's new leader. Reid endured a difficult 4-12 season during his final year in Philadelphia, but his 120 victories, .609 winning percentage, and 10 playoff victories all stood as Eagles franchise records. On Jan. 12 in consultation with Reid, Hunt would hire John Dorsey as the team's new general manager, putting in place the organization that would quickly turn the Chiefs into winners.

No move in the resurrection of the franchise looms larger than the hiring of Reid but there have been plenty of key moves large and small in the last seven years that helped build the 2019 AFC Champions.

March 13, 2013: Trading for Alex Smith

The acquisition of Smith was touchstone for the rebuilding franchise. Smith brought stability and leadership to the quarterback position, providing Reid with a player capable of implementing his West Coast offense. Smith would lead the Chiefs to four playoff berths in five seasons with Kansas City, and his mentorship would prove invaluable in the development Patrick Mahomes.

April 25, 2013: Selecting Eric Fisher No. 1 Overall

Some fans thought the Chiefs were snake-bitten for landing the first pick in the draft during what many believed to be a down year for college talent. But the Chiefs got it right in selecting Fisher from Central Michigan. Fisher overcome early struggles in his career to become a Pro Bowl left tackle and anchor for the team's offensive line.

April 26, 2013: Choosing Travis Kelce in Third Round

Kelce would miss most of his rookie season with a knee injury, but it didn't take long for him to prove himself as one of the league's most reliable tight ends. He owns the NFL record for tight ends with four-straight 1,000-yard seasons and counting.

September 1, 2013: The Second Draft

Owning the league's worst record in 2012 meant the Chiefs owned the No. 1 position in the league's waiver

Former Kansas City Chiefs general manager John Dorsey, left, poses with head coach Andy Reid during the news conference announcing Dorsey's hiring in 2013. The duo would go on to build the foundation of a championship team.

wire during the cutdown to 53 players for the opening week. Dorsey took advantage of the privilege of getting first dibs on all players released by other clubs that weekend. The Chiefs landed defensive backs Ron Parker and Marcus Cooper, linebackers Dezman Moses and James-Michael Johnson, tight end Sean McGrath, defensive lineman Jaye Howard and wide receiver Chad Hall. The group played a total of 255 game for Chiefs with 138 starts, with Parker playing with the club through 2018. None remain on the 2019 roster, but this group played a key role in the early tenure of Reid and Dorsey.

May 12, 2014: Signing Dan Sorensen

Not all NFL teams are built with high draft picks, blockbuster trades and splashy free agent deals. Old fashioned scouting and good luck are needed too, and the Chiefs found that with undrafted free agent Sorensen. He's proven a valuable backup at safety and one of the league's best special teams players.

March 9, 2016: Signing Mitchell Schwartz

The Browns unsurprisingly mangled contract negotiations with their star right tackle, and the Chiefs seized their opportunity to land Schwartz with a five-year $33 million contract. He's earned All-Pro honors in all four seasons with the Chiefs.

April 29, 2016: Drafting Chris Jones

Dorsey moved out of the first round and still got the guy he wanted in Jones with the sixth selection of the second round. Dorsey gathered two additional picks, one of which would net offensive lineman Parker Ehinger, a key piece in a future deal.

April 30, 2016: Drafting Tyreek Hill and Demarcus Robinson

The Chiefs targeted wide receivers on the third day of the draft, picking up two members of their "Legion of Zoom" in back-to-back rounds. The selection of Hill set off an initial firestorm due to character questions, but Reid and Dorsey staked their reputations on the pick.

April 27, 2017: Moving up for Patrick Mahomes

The Chiefs entered the 2017 draft targeting Mahomes, but knew he wouldn't fall to No. 27, the choice they owned in the first round. The front office gambled that Mahomes would fall to No. 10, and engineered a deal with Buffalo in exchange for two first-round picks and a third-round selection. Easily the best trade the Chiefs ever made.

July 10, 2017: Promoting Brett Veach to GM

The Chiefs shocked the NFL offseason on June 22 when the club announced it was parting ways with general manager John Dorsey. Hunt never explained in detail the reasons for letting Dorsey go – sources said communication and management issues led to the departure. Veach shared a strong relationship with Reid, and sold Hunt on his long-term plan to build a winner in Kansas City.

September 26, 2017: Harrison Butker Off the Practice Squad

The Chiefs could have found a short-term solution in light of an injury to incumbent kicker Cairo Santos. But special teams coordinator Dave Toub saw a future star in Butker, and Veach plucked the rookie off the Carolina Panthers practice squad. He set an NFL record with 426 points through his first three seasons.

March 15, 2018: Signing Free Agents Sammy Watkins and Anthony Hitchens

The beginning of free agency in 2018 marked the beginning of dramatic turnover of the roster, especially on the defensive side. The club released veteran linebacker Tamba Hali, officially concluded deals shipping out Alex Smith and cornerback Marcus Peters and brought Hitchens and Watkins into the fold. The Smith trade to Washington also brought cornerback Kendall Fuller.

Drafted in the third round out of the University of Cincinnati in the 2013 NFL Draft, Travis Kelce is one of several homegrown players on the roster to make a major impact on the franchise.

March 22, 2018: Damien Williams Signed

Adding Williams behind starter Kareem Hunt looked like a depth move at the time, but it would later prove fortuitous when the Chiefs would part ways with Hunt in November. Williams has been a primetime player for the Chiefs in the postseason.

August 31, 2018: Trade for Charvarius Ward

Veach doesn't believe any deal is small or minor, and this deal made shortly before the team's final preseason game proves that. The Chiefs sent Ehinger to Dallas for Ward, who would step into the team's starting lineup by the end of his rookie season and rank as the club's top cornerback in 2019.

January 24, 2019: Hiring Defensive Coordinator Steve Spagnuolo

Reid made a difficult decision for him in letting go of defensive coordinator Bob Sutton, but it was evident the Chiefs needed a new approach on that side of the ball. Reid's trust in Spagnuolo went a long way towards the quick rebuild of the team's defense.

March 10-14, 2019: Signing Tyrann Mathieu, Shedding Veterans

Veach further cemented his stamp on the Kansas City defense with the release of veteran linebacker Justin Houston and safety Eric Berry, and sending edge rusher Dee Ford to San Francisco in a trade. The club opened free agency aggressively, landing safety Tyrann Mathieu, defensive end Alex Okafor and linebacker Damien Wilson.

April 24, 2019: Trade for Frank Clark

Veach continued his aggressive rebuild of the team's defense in sending his 2019 first-round selection to Seattle for Clark and immediately handing him a new deal worth a franchise-record $104 million. In Clark and Mathieu, Veach landed the new leaders on his defense.

April 26, 2019: Drafting Mecole Hardman and Juan Thornhill

Veach made another splash in the second round of the draft, first picking up the speedster Hardman and seven picks later landing Thornhill, who would win a starting job beside Mathieu in Week 1. The club also landed a group of key role players in the draft, including defensive tackle Khalen Saunders and cornerback Rashad Fenton.

October 21, 2019: Signing Mike Pennel

Teams must make dozens of roster moves during the season addressing injuries and filling in holes, and Pennel proved a critical in-season addition. The Topeka, Kansas native grew up a Chiefs fan, and the 28-year-old veteran brought leadership to the locker room and toughness to the run defense. The Chiefs won nine-straight games with Pennel in the lineup

Dec. 17, 2019: Claiming Terrell Suggs off Waivers

Sometimes good fortune falls in your lap. The Arizona Cardinals waived Suggs, but the 37-year-old future Hall of Famer could have opted for retirement. Reid and Veach successfully pitched him Kansas City as a destination where he could win a second Super Bowl ring. ■

Terrell Suggs and his championship pedigree with the Ravens was the last piece to the Super Bowl puzzle for the Chiefs.

15
QUARTERBACK

Patrick Mahomes

Mahomes Spent His Offseason Trying to Get One Game Better in 2019

The 2018-2019 NFL season ended only hours before Patrick Mahomes went to work trying to figure out how to win the 2020 Super Bowl. An ill-fated defensive penalty and a coin toss prematurely ended the Chiefs' season, but Mahomes immediately went to work watching film, trying to see what he could have done to avoid a 37-31 loss to New England Patriots in the AFC Championship.

"You have to, you have to learn from those things," Mahomes explained. "You learn from every experience you get in this league, that's the biggest thing."

How does an MVP quarterback improve on near perfection? That's the challenge facing Mahomes, who entered last season as a curiosity but begins this year's campaign with a target squarely on his back. A year ago, head coach Andy Reid wanted his gunslinger to test the limits of what he could and could not do. Now, the mentor wants his pupil breaking down walls and pushing himself further.

"We are going to continue to add and build the offense, that is one thing," Reid said. "But then you have these great minds in the NFL, these defensive coordinators who have opportunities to study us. How

are they going to stop Patrick and this offense? What are they going to do? You're not going to sneak up on anybody, you know that."

When the Chiefs returned for offseason workouts in April, Reid greeted Mahomes with cutups of every throw Mahomes made last season, breaking down each situation analyzing what worked and what didn't work – along with what might work the next time.

"Z-in, here is your 20 Z-ins that you ran," Reid described his process with his passer. The 58-yard touchdown pass Mahomes delivered to Tyreek Hill in Week 1 against the Los Angeles Chargers was one of those Z-in throws. "What can we do better here? How are teams defending you? Your foot work, when you are working the back or the Z or Y, those type of things. So, you go through all of it."

Mahomes admits he made a lot of plays off-script last year, but the offseason analysis illustrated to him where he can make gains by more often taking what the defensive gives him.

"I have to keep finding that line whenever I want to try to make the big play happen and when I want to just take the easy completion, move the chains, keep

Patrick Mahomes holds the Lamar Hunt Trophy after the AFC Championship against the Tennessee Titans. The Chiefs won 35-24 to advance to Super Bowl LIV.

the offense on the field, keep rolling down the field," Mahomes said. "That's stuff that I have to keep working on every single year and that (tape) really opened my eyes to that."

Outside of the Xs and Os, however, Mahomes feels much more comfortable within his own skin. A year ago, everything he experienced proved new and at times surprising.

"Last year I was trying to become the leader, trying to figure out ways to do different stuff with different players and different teammates," Mahomes said.

Offseason workouts made it evident that Mahomes found his voice. He no longer needs to figure out how to become a leader; this offense and team unquestionably belongs to him and he now knows when to make his presence felt.

"Whenever I may see a practice starting off maybe not the right way," Mahomes said. "It's stuff like those little things where you kind of know when to talk whenever you can change a practice instead of sitting back and just letting it happen is something picked up on from last season."

Not all of Mahomes' offseason time involved football. In between offseason workouts, OTAs and minicamp, the new toast of the NFL sandwiched in sponsorship appearances, commercial shoots and the launch of his charitable foundation. That doesn't even include moving into a new house, playing golf and making buddy trips with Travis Kelce to the Final Four and the Stanley Cup.

Those are the demands on the league's reigning MVP poised to become the new face of the league, following in the footsteps of Peyton Manning and Tom Brady. Football, however, is never far from his mind.

"It's always 100 percent football, but it's a thing where it's going to definitely shut down the traveling a little bit more," Mahomes said.

Patrick Mahomes came back better than ever after falling a game short of the Super Bowl in 2019.

Mahomes doesn't set any individual statistical plateaus for himself. "Going out there and winning football games" and taking the Chiefs to the Super Bowl are all he aspires to accomplish. He showed last season he could will his team to victories at times. The AFC Championship game, however, served as a final reminder that the Chiefs' defense plays a critical role in determining how much the team needs from its quarterback.

Nine of his 50 touchdown passes came in the fourth quarter of games in which the Chiefs lost or were forced to score in the last quarter to hold off an opponent in a single-score game. Mahomes threw 12 touchdowns combined in games against Pittsburgh and the Los Angeles Rams in which a leaky Chiefs defense surrendered 91 total points.

If the Chiefs play better defense, Mahomes could easily fall short of the 5,097 yards passing and 50 touchdown throws, yet it could be a better season for him and the team. That's dandy with Mahomes if new defensive coordinator Steve Spagnuolo could develop a complementary style that turns high-scoring losses into low-scoring wins.

"The passion and the fire that he has, it's huge, and I'm going to love every bit of it of being able to go out there every single day and compete," Mahomes said of Spagnuolo, "and then having that type of guy on the sideline with us and that competitor that's going to fire everybody up every single play, every single game."

The 2018-2019 season may have started out as a learning experience for the first year starting quarterback, but he no longer holds any such illusions this season. Mahomes has only one mission.

"We need to get to the Super Bowl, that's the goal," Mahomes said. "There's no other goals, it's finding ways to win games, it's finding ways to position yourself the right way and finding ways to get to that Super Bowl and finding ways to win it when you get there." ■

Patrick Mahomes began thinking about the 2020 Super Bowl the moment the 2019 AFC Championship Game ended in disappointment for the Chiefs.

Chiefs 40, Jaguars 26
September 8, 2019 • Jacksonville, Florida

Revving the Engine

Chiefs Pick Up Where They Left Off in Rolling Over Jaguars

The 2019 edition of the Kansas City Chiefs opened up the campaign almost precisely where the club left off last season with a fast-break offense racing down field and a suspect defense struggling to get off the field.

It took quarterback Patrick Mahomes just three plays and 96 seconds to find the end zone in the new season, connecting with Sammy Watkins for a 68-yard touchdown strike on the opening drive. That helped the Chiefs build an early 10-0 lead and they never trailed en route to a 40-26 victory over the Jacksonville Jaguars.

Watkins delivered career highs with 198 receiving yards and three touchdowns while tight end Travis Kelce caught three passes for 88 yards. LeSean McCoy led the way on the ground with 81 yards on 10 carries. Mahomes finished 25-of-33 passing for 378 yards, helping the Chiefs pile up 491 yards of offense.

But it was the performance of Watkins that stood out the most to head coach Andy Reid, especially stepping up strong after Tyreek Hill exited the game with an injury.

"There were no indecisions after catches," Reid said. "He's big, he's fast and he is strong. We're moving him all over the place and he is smart, so that helps. I think that combination is what contributed to that. We asked him to play that zebra position and he didn't blink at that. He said put me in and let me go and I will do my thing. He plays inside and outside."

The "zebra" is the inside slot position in the Kansas City offense. Watkins said he's willing to play any role because he's more concerned about wins than stats.

"Usually I don't get the ball, but somehow Pat looked at me and I looked at him and I caught it and ran as fast as I could, and it felt really good," Watkins said.

The rebuilt defense under new coordinator Steve Spagnuolo struggled in its debut. The Jaguars tallied 428 yards of offense, most of them coming with after rookie quarterback Gardner Minshew replaced injured Nick Foles behind center. Minshew completed his first 13 passes and finished 22-of-25 passing for 275 yards and two scores.

But a third-quarter fumble forced by linebacker Damien Wilson and an interception by defensive end Frank Clark loomed large to Reid.

"Games like this are the toughest on the defensive line. I thought our guys battled through it and kept constant pressure. They were keeping people in to block. There are things we can do better all the way around in all three phases of our games – offense, defense and teams. I sure liked the effort. The more those guys play together and with the system, I just think the sky is the limit."

The victory, however, came at a cost. Hill suffered a sternoclavicular dislocation in his shoulder and collarbone that required emergency treatment at a Jacksonville hospital. Hill would miss the next four games with the injury.

Kansas City Chiefs' Armani Watts leaps high over Jacksonville Jaguars' Andrew Wingard to grab an onside kick during the second half of the 40-26 win.

The loss of Hill didn't slow the Chiefs offense, though. Reid said the receiving corps played well in filling the void left in Hill's absence.

"Guys played hard," Reid said. "Mecole (Hardman) stepped in and did his thing. (Demarcus Robinson) should have had a touchdown right there, got his hands pulled down, but he had an opportunity to score. Kelce had his go there. They tried to play a little man on him and he did well."

Mahomes also suffered a sprained left ankle that nearly knocked him from the game. He came up lame after a sack by Jacksonville's Yannick Ngakoue. Mahomes limped to bench with assistance from the trainers while a scuffle broke out involving Jaguars linebacker Myles Jack.

Officials ejected Jack from the game, and it took them long enough to sort out the situation that trainers were able to wrap the left ankle of Mahomes and allow him to stay in the game. The quarterback said adrenaline took over and helped him power through the injury.

"I was going out there and just playing football," Mahomes said. "Obviously, I wasn't as mobile as I usually am. But the team helped me out step-by-step as I tried to get the ball out of my hands and guys were making plays."

Reid said it was further testament to the competitive nature of his quarterback.

"He loves to play," Reid said. "I wanted to make sure I kept a close eye on him so we'll see how he does here when he's done with this. He's a tough kid, he's a competitive son of a gun." ■

Running back Damien Williams rushes for a touchdown in the win against the Jaguars. Williams had 26 yards rushing and 39 yards receiving in the game.

Chiefs 28, Raiders 10
September 15, 2019 • Oakland, California

So Long, Oakland

Kansas City Triumphs in Their Final Trip to Oakland

Chiefs wide receiver Demarcus Robinson is loved by his teammates for the little things he does on the field, but against the Oakland Raiders, head coach Andy Reid got to give him credit for the big plays he made in a 28-10 win.

"There's nobody that epitomizes do your job and don't worry about the results, don't worry about any credit or anything else," than Robinson, Reid said. "He kind of does all the dirty work. Then you know, this today, which was beautiful."

Quarterback Patrick Mahomes together with Robinson helped the Chiefs own the second quarter as they rattled off 28 unanswered points, including back-to-back drives of 95 and 94 yards. Mahomes completed 12-of-17 passing for 178 yards with four touchdowns in the quarter. Robinson contributed the lion's share of the work, catching four passes for 133 yards and two scores during the period.

Robinson didn't mind waiting for his opportunity to come. He understands the Chiefs have a plethora of offensive targets, and patience is a virtue.

"We got a lot of great guys in the room, and they've been here longer than I have," Robinson said. "Their number gets called more times than mine does, but today mine got called and I was able to make plays and show the coaches I can make plays too. Hopefully I get a couple of more plays."

Mahomes said he was happy to see Robinson have a big day.

"He's a guy that he kind of gets lost in the shuffle of things sometimes whenever he's a guy that's super talented and makes a lot of big plays happen," Mahomes said. "It's everything from catching the ball on scrambles, catching touchdowns, maybe being the last read across the middle of the field, or making the blocks and doing whatever he can to help his teammates out. When you have guys that play hard for each other and that they finally get their time to shine, it's always good to see that."

The Chiefs rolled to a victory, but it didn't come about the way Reid envisioned. Mahomes finished 30-of-44 passing for 443 yards, but most of the damage came in the explosive second quarter. Mahomes made a conscious effort to stay in the pocket while nursing the left ankle he sprained against Jacksonville.

"There were times I focused more on throwing the ball instead of running," Mahomes said. "But just trying to stay in the pocket, make things happen from there. I've got a lot of skill positions. The O-line protected really well for me and kept me upright and kept me where I could just move around the pocket and make throws."

On the ground the offense netted just 31 rushing yards on 22 carries while Oakland rookie running back Josh Jacobs racked up 99 yards on just 12 carries in leading the Raiders to 129 yards rushing. Jacobs exited the game early in the second quarter due to dehydration and didn't return until Oakland's opening possession of the third quarter.

Wide receiver Demarcus Robinson scores a touchdown as Oakland Raiders cornerback Gareon Conley looks on. Robinson had a huge game with six catches for 172 yards and two touchdowns.

Reid measured his concern with losing the battle in the trenches with his trust in his coaching staff to respond appropriately.

"Your coaches need to recognize it and then make the adjustments accordingly," Reid said. "Then you have to have confidence in that if you need to use your short-intermediate game to kind of replace the run game that you can do that if they're packing the box on you. This offense normally allows not to have to force something in there that maybe a team is working to take out and away from you. It's just a matter of recognizing it."

The worst news for the Chiefs came on the injury front with the loss of left tackle Eric Fisher. Fisher suffered a core muscle injury in practice on Friday leading up to the game and tried to give it a go. He left after just four plays and would undergo surgery later in the week, with the injury keeping him out for eight games. Running back Damien Williams also exited the game with a knee injury.

The game also marked the last trip the Chiefs will make to Oakland to play their longtime rivals. The Raiders will relocate to Las Vegas for the 2020 season. The game also marked what will likely be the last NFL game played on a dirt baseball infield. Oakland–Alameda County Coliseum is the last multipurpose stadium in use serving as home to both an NFL and Major League Baseball franchise.

Reid appreciates the history of the coliseum, but that doesn't mean he feels nostalgic about the place.

"I've only been a small part of that," Reid said. "We had some great games here. I'm not going to tell you I am going to miss it. There are some things that come with that. This year we didn't have to dodge sewage in the locker room or anything. Things that come with an older building that you have to deal with, but the tradition is pretty awesome." ■

Tight end Travis Kelce scores on a 27-yard touchdown in the first half, one of his seven catches on the day for 107 yards.

Chiefs 33, Ravens 28
September 22, 2019 • Kansas City, Missouri

MVP Who?

Mahomes Prevails in Duel with Lamar Jackson

Preparing to face Baltimore, Andy Reid dropped the gauntlet with his big men up front on both sides of the football. The Ravens play with a nasty streak in the trenches, and Reid wanted to see a little more backyard brawling than the team showed the week before in Oakland.

"In games like that when you get two big boys playing each other, it comes down to the big boys," Reid said. "You have to have the right mindset going in."

The head coach got the performance he wanted in a 33-28 win over the Ravens. The offensive line paved the way for 140 yards on the ground while surrendering just a single sack. The defensive line picked up three sacks, but most importantly held 2019 NFL MVP Lamar Jackson to just 46 yards on eight carries while pinning him in the pocket most of the game.

"It doesn't have to be pretty," Reid said. "It's not always pretty, but you've got to fight in there."

That was the mantra all week long for the linemen.

"Not everything is pretty against a defense like that," center Austin Reiter said. Left guard Andrew Wylie quickly agreed. "Definitely not. There's some ugly plays, but a win's a win. There's going to be ugly plays every game," Wylie said.

The goal, according to defensive end Frank Clark, was to make the necessary plays no matter what it looks like on film.

"I say all the time it's not perfect, but if you play the technique enough, you make those plays that you need to win the game," Clark said.

Reid's emphasis on the line play came one week after the Chiefs clearly lost the battle in the trenches to the Raiders. Oakland out gained the Chiefs 129 to 31 on the ground in Week 2. That showed too little push on the offensive side, not enough on the defensive side.

"Coach Reid put a lot of weight on the O-line's shoulder and the D-line's shoulders to step it up a little bit," Wylie said.

Early on it looked like the message may not have sunk in all the way. The Chiefs opening drive stalled out, brought to an end when left tackle Cam Erving, filling in for the injured Eric Fisher, allowed a sack to linebacker Matt Judon.

"I had kind of a rough start, just as an offense," Erving said. "Had to settle into the game a little bit, playing against a good defense. But guys are going to make plays."

The defense started turning the tide on the Ravens' first possession. Jackson drove his team 84 yards for a touchdown on the opening drive, but the line started establishing its presence. Jackson didn't find many places to run, and the Chiefs forced him to stay in the pocket for a career-high 43 passes. The Ravens did find some running room, gaining 203 yards on the ground. Most of that damage, however, came running away from the teeth of the Chiefs' defense.

Patrick Mahomes had a big day in his duel with Baltimore's Lamar Jackson, throwing for 374 yards and three touchdowns in the victory.

"They were working off of the end and in formations where they could do that," Reid said. "We were inside-conscious on a couple of those and they hit it back outside."

The Chiefs offensive line started asserting itself on the next drive. Mahomes led the team on a 76-yard drive capped off by a 1-yard touchdown run by LeSean McCoy. McCoy and backfield mate Darrel Williams contributed 39 yards on six touches during the drive.

The effort from both lines helped the Chiefs establish a 23-6 led at halftime. In the second half, it was the defensive line that started showing some breaks. The Ravens ran 78 offensive plays in the game, which left a lot of time for defensive tackle Chris Jones and company chase Jackson around the field.

"A lot of plays, a lot of running around," Jones said. "A battle. It was everything and that."

The Ravens double teamed Clark and Jones much of the game, a strategy that doesn't bother Clark at all.

"I love the double teams, they got to keep it coming, it just opens up opportunities for my other guys," Clark said.

The extra attention on Clark and Jones means others on the defensive line get one-on-one matchups. Emmanuel Ogbah has thrived in that environment, ranking second on the team in pressures as the team's top-rated edge rusher according to Pro Football Focus.

"These guys are all in and they're playing fast," Reid said. "They practice fast. They want to be the best, that's what they strive for. You see them hustling, they're studying extra."

Yet the Ravens mounted a furious rally in the second half, reeling off 22 points and 294 yards of offense. That included 119 yards on the ground, which frustrated Jones.

"As a defense, you don't like that," Jones said. "You kind of have to be consistent with it, especially on defense when you got the lead coming out of halftime.

You want to put your foot on their throat and just dominate the game right there. I feel like we kind of let them back into the game."

It was a play from the defensive line, however, that proved pivotal to sealing the win. On third-and-10 from the Kansas City 16-yard line, Clark picked up his first sack with the Chiefs, snuffing out the Ravens drive. That held Baltimore to a field goal, and helped provide the winning margin.

"We kept getting after it, we kept putting pressure on as the end of the game came," Clark said. "We put more pressure on (Jackson) to force some mistakes, and we got off the field."

After the final whistle, players in both position groups sported weary smiles in the locker room.

"We knew they were going to come hard," Wylie said of the Ravens. "They're a great team. It's a feeling – this is one that's sweet, sweet coming into the locker room after a hard one like this. It's awesome."

They also took satisfaction in knowing they met the challenge Reid issued them during the week.

"Glad we could make dad proud," Wylie said with a grin.

But there was also wariness knowing challenges remain ahead. Next week brings a trip to the surprisingly undefeated Detroit Lions, who also feature a stout offensive line and a front seven with size.

"We're going to get everybody's best," Reiter said. "People are always coming for us." ∎

Defensive end Frank Clark sacks Lamar Jackson, part of an admirable effort by the Chiefs defense to contain the superstar quarterback.

HEAD COACH

Andy Reid

Taking Chiefs to the Super Bowl Turned Critics into Fans

Heading into Super Bowl LIV and finding someone not rooting for Andy Reid was akin to finding football's Grinch with a heart two sizes too small. After nearly 20 years of hearing criticisms for his clock management and his temperament in big games, suddenly Reid became America's sweetheart.

For Reid, who always seems to downplay both compliments and critiques, the sudden outpouring of support from around the league was humbling.

"I appreciate all of that," Reid said when asked about the support from many of his former players and coaches. "They know how I'm wired. I do appreciate it, but they also know that I'm getting ready for the game. It's that time where there are a lot of outside influences that take place, so you have to stay focused on it. When it's all said and done, then you deal with all of that. Right now, you try to stay with as much tunnel vision as possible. But I do appreciate all of that. People have reached out and said that it's great and an unbelievable experience."

It's also not as if Reid never won a championship. He already owned a Super Bowl ring from his time with the Green Bay Packers. He served as tight ends and assistant offensive line coach for the 1996 Super Bowl winners. The following season he took over as Brett Favre's position coach but fell short in a second trip to the Super Bowl against John Elway's Denver Broncos.

Reid is also the coach that colleagues around the league look toward for inspiration. New Orleans Saints coach Sean Payton once said he watches tapes of Reid's offense every week. Chicago Bears coach Matt Nagy, a former pupil of Reid, says it's easy for him to pick up his phone at midnight and call his mentor for advice.

"We've done that a few times, and it means a lot to me because he's very authentic," Nagy said. "When you're with him every single day for all those years I was in his office, in his room, just always talking, talking ball, talking life, then when you're away from it, you really realize how much you miss it."

Tennessee Titans head coach Mike Vrabel says there's no argument about Reid's legacy in the NFL.

"Andy is a great coach," Vrabel said. "This league is better off because Andy Reid is a part of it and has coached great teams and he's prepared coaches to be head coaches. He's been a great mentor for me."

Chiefs offensive coordinator Eric Bieniemy played running back for Reid in 1999, his first season as head coach. He believes the criticism Reid gets for falling short in big games is unfair.

"For coach to be in as many championship games that

Kansas City Chiefs head coach Andy Reid arrives for Opening Night for the week of Super Bowl LIV.

he has been in – he maybe hasn't quite gotten over the hurdle yet – I say it is still a huge accomplishment because he is still one of the best in the business," Bieniemy said.

Bieniemy doesn't believe most people understand how difficult winning a Super Bowl is.

"The last time I went to a Super Bowl was with the San Diego Chargers in the 1994 season," he said. "You don't get these opportunities all the time."

Despite the lack of success in previous championship games, Reid never felt sorry for himself.

"I look more at the disappointment for the other teams that I've been able to coach and how those kids felt, because they worked their tails off for that amount of time, and the other coaches."

It's a close race for quarterback Patrick Mahomes whether he would be happier for himself or for his coach if they win a Super Bowl together.

"Probably be happier for him for sure," Mahomes laughed. "I think I'll be pretty happy too for myself."

Chiefs chairman and CEO Clark Hunt sees parallels in between the Reid and the Hunt family. Going 50 years between Super Bowl appearances brings its own share of criticisms. But Hunt sees Reid having a universal base of support.

"Andy's a unique individual in the context of the National Football League that he has so many friends, so many people who pull for him," Hunt said. "That's not just people who were associated with the Eagles organization. I think it's a lot of coaches and teams that he competed against because he's so well respected. Just seeing that outpouring of love that I've seen for him having this opportunity speaks volumes about the kind of person he is."

Only one person on the Kansas City coaching staff has been around the coach for his entire life. That

Andy Reid finally clinched another Super Bowl berth with the AFC Championship victory, ending a 15-year drought after his appearance in Super Bowl XXXIX with the Eagles.

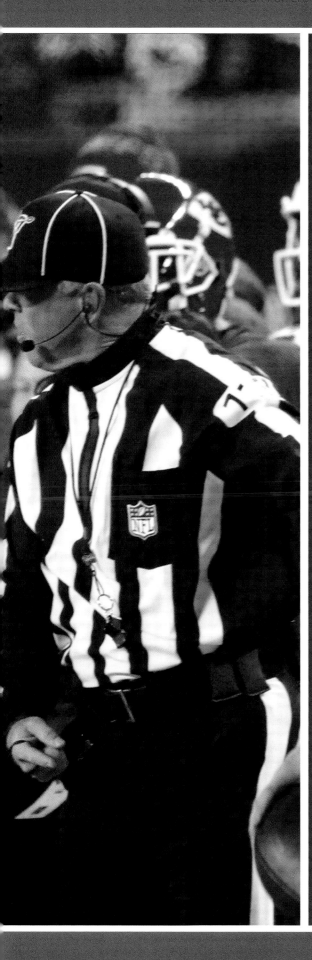

would be linebackers/outside linebackers coach Britt Reid, the coach's son.

"It's different, it's unique balancing the two," Britt said about working with his dad. "But to me it's so cool because you grow up as a coach's kid, you don't really know what goes on behind the scenes. You don't get to see your dad all that much. Now I get to make up for that."

Winning the Super Bowl would be a moment of celebration for the entire family, he says.

"I think everyone wants it for him," Britt said. "Players, coaches, everybody. It would be awesome."

Chiefs special teams coordinator Dave Toub's friendship with Reid goes back to 1987 when they worked together on Bob Stull's staff at Texas-El Paso. The pair left with Stull for Missouri in 1989, and Reid brought him to Philadelphia in 2001. They've worked together for seven seasons in Kansas City.

Toub says no one deserves a Super Bowl championship more than his friend Andy. He's given a lot of thought to what it would feel like to be on the field watching Reid accept the Lombardi Trophy.

"To not have a Super Bowl win under his belt – this would be huge," Toub said. "I don't know if I'd stop crying with him. I'd probably hug him forever. I'm just so proud of what he's done and everything he's done in his career and he needs that. He needs this. He needs that," Toub repeated. ■

Andy Reid won over many of his critics on his way to finally leading the Chiefs to an elusive second Super Bowl triumph for the franchise, the first in Reid's storied head coaching career.

Chiefs 34, Lions 30
September 29, 2019 • Detroit, Michigan

Rocky Road in Detroit
Chiefs Overcome a Myriad of Mistakes in Remaining Unbeaten

The Chiefs defensive coordinator Steve Spagnuolo preaches to his team every day in practice the importance of finishing the play. You never know when scooping a loose ball up off the turf and racing to the end zone when the play appears over might pay dividends. That's exactly what went through the mind of Bashaud Breeland in the middle of a wild third quarter in Detroit.

"Coach Spags preach that every day," Breeland said. "Pick the ball up, whether it's live or dead, we never know. We always pick it up and let the chips fall where they may."

The Lions benefitted from a face mask penalty on defensive tackle Xavier Williams that set them up with a first-and-goal at the 1-yard line. Running back Kerryon Johnson carried the ball towards the end zone on target to give his team the go-ahead score in a 13-13 game.

Johnson plowed into the pile in and tried to stretch the ball across the goal line as he fell to the ground. Williams swiped at the ball and managed to knock it free, then landed on the ball but couldn't corral it.

"I saw it down, I didn't hear no whistle," Breeland said. "I saw my teammate picked it up and he kind of put it back down. I stared at him, so I just picked it up and ran with it. Just hoped that it wasn't down."

Breeland streaked 100 yards to the opposite end zone escorted by Tyrann Mathieu, himself not sure exactly what happened.

"I actually initially made the tackle, so I was at the bottom of the pile," Mathieu said. "I didn't know what was going on, I just saw white jerseys running and I got up and tried to meet them in the end zone."

Officials huddled on the field and eventually ruled the play a fumble and a clear recovery by the Chiefs resulting in a touchdown. A replay review upheld the call on the field.

That wasn't the only wild play in a third quarter taking 53 minutes to complete. Both teams exchanged fumbles on the first four drives of the period and combined for five lost fumbles. Detroit started three of its four third-quarter drives on the positive side of the field resulting in only a touchdown and a field goal. The Chiefs defense found itself constantly defending its own end zone.

"It's hard to play defense like that," Mathieu said. I think they scored one time, but we held up pretty well."

Despite the constant turnovers and defensive stands, it was an offensive drive that eventually put the game away for the Chiefs.

Patrick Mahomes, still dealing with a sore left ankle and missing key starters on offense including Tyreek Hill and Eric Fisher, didn't look his MVP best against the Lions. He finished the game 24-42 passing for 315 yards and no touchdowns. But Mathieu said the Chiefs had confidence Mahomes would engineer a game-winning drive at the end.

"His demeanor doesn't change whether we're up by 30 or down by 10 points," Mathieu said. "It feels good to have a quarterback like that, and like I said, it goes throughout the locker room, it goes through the team,

Patrick Mahomes scrambles during the first half of a close win over the Lions. Mahomes had 315 yards passing and 54 yards rushing in the game.

we always feel like we got a shot."

Tight end Travis Kelce concurred.

"No matter how long it takes us to get it there, whether it's one play or 16 plays, 20 plays, it doesn't matter," Kelce said. "We're going north, and we're getting that ball in that end zone, and I think Pat does an unbelievable job of rallying the troops when we need it most."

It took 13 plays in just 2 minutes, 6 seconds, but Mahomes got the job done. A 15-yard scramble on fourth-and-8 from the Chiefs' 34-yard line extended the drive, and Mahomes completed 6-of-9 passing for 55 yards on the game-winning drive.

Mahomes delivered a brief message of encouragement to his teammates on the final drive: "Be who you are."

"It's not about someone having to do something spectacular, it's not about someone having to do and be more than themselves," Mahomes said. "It's about believing in each other and just being who we are and then letting everything fall in line whenever you follow those footsteps."

That message resonated, Kelce said. Mahomes connected with five different receivers on the final drive.

"We have faith in every single one of the guys in that locker room, Kelce said. "It doesn't matter who it is or what they're doing. We have Patrick Mahomes back there slinging that rock."

Backup running back Darrel Williams punched the ball in from the 1-yard line with 20 seconds remaining, with a helpful shove from center Austin Reiter.

"Being on the 1-yard line as a running back, you shouldn't be denied," Williams said. "I was trying not to get denied and I know for sure I had to put the team on my back and get in there, and do whatever it takes to get in there."

The final score, like the game itself, wasn't a work of art. Yet the Chiefs moved to 4-0, joining the Patriots as the only undefeated teams in the AFC.

"It wasn't pretty, but we got it done," Breeland said. ■

The Chiefs defense breaks up the Hail Mary at the end of the game in their uncomfortably close victory over Detroit.

Colts 19, Chiefs 13
October 6, 2019 • Kansas City, Missouri

Limping Away

Mahomes Tweaks Ankle Again as Scoring Streak Ends in Loss

The rash of injuries riddling the Chiefs finally caught up with them against the Indianapolis Colts, with Patrick Mahomes limping off the field at one point and four other Chiefs starters leaving the contest including defensive tackle Chris Jones in a 19-13 loss on Sunday Night Football.

Mahomes limped off the field late in the first half, emerging after halftime with a freshly wrapped left ankle. It was the same ankle Mahomes sprained in Week 1 against Jacksonville and that had continued to limit his mobility. One of his offensive linemen also accidentally stepped on the ankle late in the third quarter.

"Just re-aggravated it a little bit there in the first half, and then got stepped on in the second half," Mahomes said. "Obviously it's going to be a little sore tomorrow. For me, just kind of going into treatment and getting it better so I can be prepared for next week."

The 13 points scored by the Chiefs ended the club's streak of 20-straight regular-season games scoring more than 25 points. The streak stretched 22 games including postseason contests. Both streaks are NFL records.

Mahomes finished the game 22-of-39 passing for 321 yards and a touchdown. He was 2-of-4 for 43 yards with a 14-yard scramble on the team's final drive. He couldn't escape the Colts' pass rush on his final play of the game, however, absorbing his fourth sack of the contest with 1:19 remaining in the game.

Mahomes said he never considered leaving the game.

"I was going to battle through regardless," Mahomes said. "We were in a hard-fought game. For us it wasn't going our way, but I felt like we still had a chance, so I was going to find a way to get through the rest of the game."

The Chiefs endured a plethora of other injuries throughout the contest, starting from the beginning of the game. Wide receiver Sammy Watkins exited for good on the team's first drive with a hamstring injury. The Chiefs also lost linebacker Anthony Hitchens with a groin injury and left guard Andrew Wylie with a sprained ankle.

But it was injuries along the defensive line that inflicted the most damage. The team finished the game with just five healthy defensive linemen, pressing rookie Khalen Saunders into action for his first NFL game. Jones suffered a groin injury that would keep him out of action for three weeks, while defensive tackle Xavier Williams landed on injured reserve with a high-ankle sprain that kept him out of the lineup until January.

The lone bright spot came from the latest Chiefs receiver to post a career day. Second-year receiver Byron Pringle hauled in six catches for 103 yards along with his first NFL touchdown. The former Kansas State Wildcat entered the contest with two catches for 20 yards in the first four games of his professional career.

Pringle's biggest showcase moment came on Kansas City's second drive. The Chiefs faced a third-and-18 from the Indianapolis 27-yard line. Mahomes immediately felt pressure and scrambled nearly all the way to midfield before reversing course.

Mahomes bolted back toward the line of scrimmage, letting loose a dart from around the 30-yard line that found its way into the waiting hands of Pringle in the end zone for a touchdown.

"One thing about Mahomes, you just stay alive and keep moving because he will find you, anywhere on the

Patrick Mahomes re-aggravated an ankle injury in the first loss of the season for the Chiefs.

field," Pringle said. "Even if you were in the stands."

The big day came after a series of stops and starts for Pringle in his football career. He seemingly clinched a spot on the 53-man roster last season as an undrafted rookie before a torn hamstring in the preseason finale sent him to injured reserve. He made the active roster this season, but the team waived him Sept. 10 to make room for the return of receiver De'Anthony Thomas. Four days later, he returned to the roster.

Through it all, Pringle recalled one of the rules taught to him in college by former Kansas State head coach Bill Snyder – don't give up.

"I always keep a positive mindset even when I'm down," Pringle said. "I've been in tougher situations and overcome adversity. I just always keep a positive mindset and smile at the end of the day."

After Pringle's touchdown, the Chiefs offense went into one of its prepared group celebrations. Hardman, Robinson and tight end Travis Kelce joined Pringle for the Macarena dance in the end zone.

"We planned it during the week," Pringle said. "I didn't know how to do that, man."

That was the only thing it looked like he didn't have down pat on Sunday night. ∎

Texans 31, Chiefs 24
October 13, 2019 • Kansas City, Missouri

Out of Time

Texans Play Keep Away But Hill Makes Strong Return

The Chiefs declined to put a timetable on the return of Tyreek Hill after the receiver suffered a sternoclavicular dislocation against Jacksonville in Week 1 yet almost no one expected him to return as quickly and as strong as he did in Week 6 against Houston.

Patrick Mahomes took a shot deep toward Hill on the team's opening offensive play. They didn't connect there, but they did team up on five catches for 80 yards and two touchdowns.

That was about the only bright spot for Andy Reid and the Chiefs in a 31-24 loss to Houston.

"It was good to get him back out there," Reid said. "That was a positive, to have him back out there and come out healthy."

Hill's return helped the Chiefs jump out of the blocks quickly against the Texans. The offense moved down the field in a six-play, 91-yard opening drive capped with a 46-yard touchdown strike from Mahomes to Hill.

Two penalties left the Chiefs dealing with a third-and-21 at the Houston 46-yard line. Mahomes saw Texans linebacker Whitney Mercilus jump across the line of scrimmage.

"We had an offside play, and instead of going for maybe trying to get the goal range, know I had the free play," Mahomes said. "I put it up there for Tyreek and he made a great play."

Hill said he just wanted to make a play for his quarterback.

"I'm going to do whatever it takes to make him look the best," Hill said. "That's my dog, that's my boy, so if he throws it up, I tell each and every one of the receivers that's our ball, it don't matter if it's five people around, four or one, we're going to get the ball."

The euphoria, however, didn't last long. The Texans rallied in the second quarter to assume a 23-17 lead at halftime. Hill and Mahomes hooked up one more time for a 6-yard touchdown score with 6:30 left to put the Chiefs back up front 24-23.

The Texans took control after that point, playing keep away from the Chiefs. Kansas City ran just six plays and netted only 2 yards over the final 21 1/2 minutes of the game. Hill couldn't explain what happened in the second half.

"I'm just out there running my routes, doing my thing," Hill said. "That's what I tell my guys, control what we can control, so that's what we do."

The Chiefs set a new club record they would have preferred not to reach against the Texans, holding the ball for just 20 minutes, 12 seconds. That's the least time of possession the Chiefs have ever had in a regular-season home game.

The previous low came in Week 10 of the 1985 season when the Chiefs held the ball for just 20 minutes, 14 seconds in a 36-28 loss to Pittsburgh. The Chiefs finished 6-10 that season.

The Chiefs ran 36 passing plays compare to just 11 rushes, which Reid said resulted from the team's run-

Wide receiver Tyreek Hill does a flip as he celebrates a touchdown during the second half of the loss to the Texans. Hill had five catches for 80 yards and two touchdowns in the game.

pass option plays tending toward the pass.

"That's some of what you do when you're in an RPO game," Reid said. "If you're doing that then you'll have some that end up being throws. That's how we roll. We'll go back and look at it and see what we need to do better there. That starts with me."

Hill expects the Chiefs to bounce back from the adversity that comes from dropping back-to-back games at home.

"We're the Chiefs, that's what we do," Hill said. "We got the MVP quarterback, the best tight end in the league, the best offensive line in the league my opinion, so we're just going to keep building off that." ∎

Chiefs 30, Broncos 6
October 17, 2019 • Denver, Colorado

Disaster Avoided

Mahomes' Knee Injury Momentarily Derails Chiefs' Super Bowl Dreams

Chiefs fans received their wish when Andy Reid kept his offense on the field for a fourth-and-1 at the Denver 5-yard line but it didn't take long for elation to turn to dread. Patrick Mahomes lined up under center for the most innocuous of plays, the quarterback sneak. "Not too many people get hurt on sneaks," said Andy Reid after the game. But this time something happened. Mahomes pushed for the first down and became tangled up in the crowd of blockers and would-be tackles. Mahomes got twisted up at the bottom of the pile, the right knee buckled.

Wide receiver Tyreek Hill said he knew something was wrong immediately.

"I kind of couldn't believe it at first," Hill said. "And then when I actually saw his knee, I kind of want to pray for him, because Pat is the hardest working dude in our locker room. You never want to see that, especially from our quarterback."

Tight end Travis Kelce said Mahomes didn't appear in too much pain, but it was evident something was wrong with his right knee.

"I saw his knee, it didn't look like a knee," Kelce said. "It was all out of whack, I couldn't even describe it. You just looked at it, you were like, there's something wrong with him."

Once the team's physician and athletic trainers conducted a further examination, Mahomes realized they dodged a bullet. Mahomes suffered a dislocation of the right kneecap but no break or damaged ligaments. The medical staff credited the "elasticity" of Mahomes ligaments and tendons as a reason for the lack of more severe damage.

Indeed, the injury would be short term – Mahomes would actually practice in limited duty the following week and missed only two games before returning to action.

On the field in Denver that Thursday night, the results were far less dramatic. Mahomes left early in the second quarter with the Chiefs leading 10-6. Facing another fourth-and-1 from the 1-yard line, Reid didn't gamble this time; Harrison Butker hit a 20-yard field goal to put the Chiefs ahead 13-6.

From there the Kansas City defense took over. On the first play of Denver's next drive, linebacker Anthony Hitchens drilled quarterback Joe Flacco and popped the ball loose. Fellow linebacker Reggie Ragland scooped up the ball at the 5-yard line and went into the end zone, putting the Chiefs up 20-6.

The defense sacked Flacco nine times, the third-most sacks in a game in franchise history. Reid said he saw signs of new scheme and new additions finally clicking and coming up with a breakthrough performance.

"You talk about all those stats like the red zone and the quarterback ratings and all the things that go with it, but it doesn't mean much until it all comes together, and tonight it did," Reid said. "Now, it's important to

Patrick Mahomes leaves the game in the first half after injuring his right knee on a quarterback sneak.

continue building on that and that will be the challenge as we go forward. This isn't the end of the season, so we've got to just keep going."

Ragland picked up a sack of his own to go along with the fumble return for a touchdown. He said the defense knew Flacco would hold on to the ball longer than most other quarterbacks, and they planned to attack that weakness.

"We are just doing what got us here, what got us in this situation and what got us into the league," Ragland said. "Just playing football and having fun, that's the main thing. You can't do too much. Just have fun with it, and that's what we did tonight."

The Chiefs would also have to face life without Mahomes for a few games. Backup Matt Moore struggled out of the gate coming in for Mahomes, completing 8-of-15 passing for just 49 yards. Until he found Tyreek Hill, however, as Moore and Hill connected on a wheel route for a 57-yard touchdown to extend the Chiefs' lead.

Moore was coaching high school football at his alma mater in late August when Chad Henne fractured his right ankle in a preseason game against San Francisco. Less than nine weeks later he would start in place of Mahomes in the league's most explosive offense.

"It's hard to do really the whole thing he's done, just coming in late to us when Chad got hurt and then asking him to pick up this offense, which is pretty complicated," Reid said. "He's a pro, and he's done a very nice job with it. And then it's hard to be a relief pitcher, but he's done it before. There's a certain way to prep for that, and he understands that and it paid off for him." ∎

Backup quarterback Matt Moore came in off the bench to help lead the Chiefs to a 30-6 win over the Broncos.

The Legion of Zoom

Dynamic Offense Built on Speed, Competition

The Arrowhead crowd erupted into cheers as Damien Williams burst into the secondary on his way to a 91-yard touchdown run that would put Kansas City on top of Minnesota 17-16. It was a game-breaking play the Chiefs needed at a big moment.

Suddenly the roar of cheers turned into roars of laughter. Wide receiver Tyreek Hill raced down the field, sped past the final would-be-tackler, caught up with Williams and passed him into the end zone.

"I told him if we had like 5 more yards, I would have stripped the ball from him and then took his touchdown," Hill said with a laugh.

That's the spirit of the Legion of Zoom.

When the Chiefs showed up to training camp for the 2019 season, one thing became quickly apparent. This team is ridiculously fast.

"This is probably the best 7-on-7 football team ever," safety Tyrann Mathieu said.

Hill is the unquestionable speed demon of the group. He ran a 4.24 40-yard dash time at his pro day in college and finished fifth in the 200 meters at the NCAA Division Indoor track and field championships in 2014.

The addition of Mecole Hardman added to the legend. The 5-10, 187-pound Hardman delivered a 4.33 40-yard time at the NFL Combine. He ran the leadoff leg for Georgia's 4x100-meter relay team that finished sixth in the 2017 SEC Championships.

Sammy Watkins (4.43), Williams (4.45) and Byron Pringle (4.46) can motor as well. Demarcus Robinson seems almost turtle speed with his deceptively fast 4.59 speed.

But the Chiefs' Legion of Zoom isn't all about speed. Their competitive fire when it comes to racing is only matched by their willingness to work together and push each other to improve, according to wide receivers coach Greg Lewis.

"Those guys are giving techniques to the younger guys that they've used or that they've seen other guys use and helping them along the way," Lewis said. "I can coach you so much. You hear it from your peers, guys respond differently to that, and it's been a big positive for our group."

Lewis' own competitive fire seems a good fit for the Legion of Zoom. First of all, he hates the name.

"Everybody in the NFL is fast," Lewis said. "We have a lot of fast guys here. I'm not big on nicknames, I'm just big on execution when we get out there and we get an opportunity to play. That's what I want. We can worry about nicknames for other people."

Secondly, he practices what he preaches. In 2009 while with Minnesota, Lewis was on the receiving end of a game-winning touchdown pass from Brett Favre that the NFL ranked No. 67 on its 100 greatest plays of all time. That play deeply influenced how he coaches his receivers today. He recalls only playing two snaps before getting pressed into service on the game-winning play.

"That's sort of how I treat our guys," Lewis explained. "The next man up. You have to be ready and prepared and you have to prepare yourself as a starter each and

Tyreek Hill is the fastest of the offensive group with a 4.24 40-yard dash time at his pro day in college, a best in the vaunted Legion of Zoom.

every day because you don't know when your number is going to be called, and then just make the play when you get opportunity. It's simple as that for me."

Lewis remains proud of playing his part in an historic moment, but the memory brings back bittersweet feelings. That Vikings season ended in the NFC Championship game with a 31-28 overtime loss to the eventual Super Bowl champion New Orleans Saints.

"We lost and we didn't win when we wanted to," Lewis said. "But OK."

That desire to improve resonates throughout the receiving corps. Quarterback Patrick Mahomes gets receivers together during the offseason and even during the bye week to run routes and catch balls. Hill gathers his fellow receivers during the offseason to run drills designed to improve strength and agility.

He also spent the past few offseasons working with a private instructor, former Nebraska receivers coach Keith Williams. He works with Williams on route running, creativity with routes and "how to be a magician" on the field, but the work extends off the field as well.

"He's taught me how to play the game and just being a man outside of football," Hill said. "Keith is a real family man, he has a wife, he has kids. Every time I go see Keith, it's about ball but it's about life after ball and who you want to be and what you want your legacy to be whenever you retire. We always talk about that, hone on that every time I go."

Striving for a legacy is what truly motivates the Chiefs offensive speed merchants. According to Lewis, it's Hill's willingness to become a leader by example that helped the receiving corps become something more than just a bunch of fast guys.

"He's detailing his work up as well, the small details of running routes, getting in and out of breaks," Lewis said. "We all know that he can run fast and get behind people but the nuances of running routes, he's really expanded his game on that part of it. And then he's touching some of the young guys the same things." ■

The Legion of Zoom has a friendly competition about who is the fastest and genuinely have fun playing the game, as Tyreek Hill (10) and Damien Williams (26) can attest to.

Packers 31, Chiefs 24
October 27, 2019 • Kansas City, Missouri

Too Many Mistakes

Miscues Prove Costly as Chiefs Drop Third-Straight Home Game

For a moment it wasn't clear if Chiefs head coach Andy Reid planned to punt or leave his offense on the field. His team faced a fourth-and-3 on its own 40-yard line with 5:13 to play against the Green Bay Packers.

But Reid sent his punt team on the field, and his offense never saw the ball again in a 31-24 loss to the Green Bay Packers. The Chiefs fell to 5-3 with the loss, their third setback in four games at Arrowhead Stadium this season.

"You can be questioned either way with it," Reid said. "I chose to do what I did there and thought it was the right thing to do at that time. It didn't necessarily pay off the way that I was hoping."

The Chiefs played an uneven second half up to that point. The defense had allowed scores on all three Packers drives in the second half, but the Chiefs were coming fresh off a 10-play, 70-yard scoring drive on their previous possession to tie the game at 24-24. The Packers responded with a two-play scoring drive, capped off with a 67-yard touchdown pass from Aaron Rodgers to Aaron Jones.

Quarterback Matt Moore faced a third-and-8 at the Kansas City 24-yard line starting the drive, finding tight end Travis Kelce for a 9-yard gain. Running back Damien Williams rushed for seven yards on two carries, bringing up a third-and-3 from the 40-yard line. Moore again looked for Kelce but couldn't connect.

Kelce took the blame for the third down failure. He finished the game with four catches on eight targets for 63 yards and a touchdown, but also had a second touchdown catch go through his hands.

"I just got to be better for Matty Moore there at the end, coming back to the ball, better for my teammates," Kelce said. "I'm just disgusted with how I played."

Moore wanted to try again, but understands he missed his opportunity on third down.

"You want to convert and stay on there, especially with how the game was going," Moore said. "I think we all knew that was a crucial situation, and we came up short. Obviously that's something we'll look at. We needed that one to stay on the field there for sure."

But after the Chiefs showed a moment of indecision on fourth down, Reid sent out Dustin Colquitt to punt. The head coach steadfastly maintains that he bases his fourth-down decisions as much on the flow of the game as the analytics of the situation.

"Some of it is feel, some of it is momentum and all those things you look at," Reid said.

The Chiefs are an offensive team, but with the game on the line Reid leaned on his defense.

"Our defense had been playing well throughout the night," Reid said. "I had confidence in them that we'd get the ball back with good field position."

It briefly looked as if Reid had made the perfect call. Colquitt's boot landed inside the 20-yard line and rolled down the 2-yard line where cornerback Rashad Fenton downed it. The Chiefs defense had held the Packers' running backs to just 13 rushes for 58 yards on the night thus far, and now the Green Bay offense needed to pound the ball on the ground.

The Packers used running backs Aaron Jones and Jamaal Williams for seven-straight run plays, grinding out 31 yards, including a 4-yard run by Jones on a third-

Aaron Rodgers and the Packers outdueled the Chiefs and sent them to their third-straight loss at Arrowhead Stadium.

and-2 conversion from the 10-yard line.

Linebacker Anthony Hitchens felt frustrated the defense couldn't come up with a play when it needed to the most.

"We all know they're going to run the ball, and we got them to third down and we couldn't get off the field," Hitchens said.

The Chiefs defense played solidly to that point, albeit yielding two back-breaking catches for 117 yards to Jones out of the backfield that led to two scores. After giving up 131 yards to the Packers in the first quarter, the Chiefs held them to just 243 yards the remainder of the game.

But injuries appeared to take their toll late, especially up front. The Chiefs started the game without Frank Clark and Chris Jones on the defensive line, then lost Alex Okafor in the second half. That left the Chiefs with just five defensive linemen at the end of the game.

"We got to get the numbers back up, get guys healthy back in there," Reid said. "We never use that as an excuse, but as you get the numbers up you can keep your rotation going. In the fourth quarter that helps you out."

On the final decisive play, the Packers faced third-and-5 from their own 33-yard line following the 2-minute warning. Green Bay went with an empty backfield, putting the game in the hands of Rodgers. He found Jones for a short pass to the right, and Jones took it 8 yards for the first down.

Hitchens said the formation didn't surprise him, but the Chiefs still couldn't stop it.

"If I was a coach, I'd do the same thing," Hitchens said. "Put your trust in Aaron Rodgers and their guys to get it done. That's what they did."

The end of this game shares some similarities with the Chiefs' 31-24 loss to Houston at Arrowhead Stadium two weeks ago. The Chiefs faced a much-less favorable fourth-and-13 from their own 22-yard line with 5:12 left in the game. Again, Reid chose to punt, the Chiefs failed to get a stop on fourth-and-3 at the 2-minute warning, and they never saw the ball again.

Reid said too many mistakes hurt the Chiefs against Green Bay.

"They come back and get you a little bit," Reid said. "It's all part of the game. We can all do better, so we make up the difference. We had opportunities to make up the difference, we didn't take care of it." ∎

Chiefs 26, Vikings 23
November 3, 2019 • Kansas City, Missouri

Viking Conquest

Backup QB Matt Moore Breaks Home Losing Streak

Harrison Butker is a serious kicker – maybe too serious, he admits – so there's an irony that the meticulous perfectionist sent a knuckleball through the uprights from 44 yards out in lifting the Chiefs to a 26-23 victory over the Minnesota Vikings in Week 9.

"I know I hit some ground before I hit the ball, and usually if I hit ground, the ball still has end-over-end rotation," Butker said. "It was kind of going crazy, but it was going straight so it's just is it going to have the distance or not. Luckily it did."

On a day when wide receiver Tyreek Hill caught six passes for 140 yards and running back Damien Williams rushed for 125, each scoring a touchdown, it was Butker who kept the Chiefs in the game until he put them over the top. Butker hit four field goals in all, connecting from 24, 45, 54 and 44 yards.

The 45-yard field goal late in the third quarter put the Chiefs ahead 20-16. A week ago, in the 31-24 loss to Green Bay, Butker left a 50-yard field wide left under similar circumstances. When the Chiefs practiced indoors on Wednesday due to cold, wintry conditions, Butker went over to Arrowhead Stadium with long snapper James Winchester and holder Dustin Colquitt to work on kicks from that exact position.

"That's why when I made the 45-yarder right hash, right to left wind, the same kick I missed last game, it was a right hash, left-to-right wind, so I was really pumped up I made that."

Butker's final two field goals came with just 2:30 remaining in the game. Colquitt called it "unreal" watching Butker connect on both kicks in what he described as the windiest day he's seen on the field in 15 seasons at Arrowhead Stadium.

"For kicking, in general, it's hard to do that on days like today," Colquitt said. "He stuck with it, kept his head down, hit two big kicks for us."

Andy Reid tipped his hat to Butker for hitting two tough kicks in unfavorable conditions for a kicker.

"That last one was as clutch as you can get," Reid said.

Butker paced the sideline before the final kick. "I was jacked up," after hitting the 54-yard field goal to tie the game. He paced the sideline, took a few deep breaths and kicked a couple of balls into the net trying to calm himself down.

"I think that's when I do the best is when I'm just kind of in my own zone," Butker said.

The game-winning kick, however, almost didn't get there. Vikings defensive end Danielle Hunter hurdled over long snapper James Winchester and appeared to get a fingertip on the ball, sending it on an unorthodox trajectory.

Backup quarterback Matt Moore threw for 275 yards and a touchdown in the close win over the Vikings.

"I thought I heard it blocked," Butker said. "A lot of O-linemen said they thought they heard it get blocked, and I looked up and the ball wasn't going end over end."

After the kick sailed through the uprights, Butker sprinted toward the other end of the field. "I think that's just from my soccer background growing up," Butker explained, "when guys scored goals they just sprint the other way."

Halfway toward the other end of the field, Butker was greeted by an exuberant Patrick Mahomes. Knee injury or not, the quarterback raced on the field to celebrate with Butker.

"I saw Patrick and I wanted to embrace him, but I'm like, 'No, he can't get hurt,'" Butker said with a laugh.

Instead, wide receiver Tyreek Hill implored Butker to head toward the end zone and jump into the crowd. That was fun, Butker admitted.

"Just so happy for this team to get a big win," he said. "We're moving forward with a lot of momentum."

Backup quarterback Matt Moore finished 23-of-35 passing for 275 yards and a touchdown in picking up his first victory as a starter in relief of Patrick Mahomes. ■

Wide receiver Sammy Watkins stretches for the catch during the second half of the win over Minnesota. Watkins had seven catches for 63 yards in the game.

Titans 35, Chiefs 32
November 10, 2019 • Nashville, Tennessee

Titanic Collapse

Mahomes Returns but Chiefs Blow Lead at Tennessee

Two games away from action didn't seem to slow Patrick Mahomes, as the Chiefs quarterback turned in a sizzling highlight-reel performance despite the team's 35-32 loss to the Tennessee Titans Sunday.

Mahomes completed 36-of-50 passing for 446 yards and three touchdowns, reporting no ill effects from the dislocated right knee that sidelined him for the last two games.

"The knee's feeling fine, just as we expected going into the game," Mahomes said. "A credit to those trainers and the training staff getting me ready to play. But the knee feels fine, and I was glad to get through another game."

Mahomes emerging healthy served as one of the lone bright spots out of the game for head coach Andy Reid.

"He did some good things," Reid said. "He came out healthy. He'll tell you the same thing, we've all got to do a little bit better, but I was happy with the things that he did for the most part."

The Chiefs offense opened the game with Mahomes rolling out to his right and delivering a deep ball for receiver Tyreek Hill was nearly intercepted by Titans safety Kenny Vaccaro. After that near disaster, Mahomes settled into a groove using the offense's run-pass options, screen passes and other quick throws to move the ball in building an early 10-0 advantage.

"That was the game plan," Mahomes said. "They played a lot of shell coverage, so we were just taking what they gave us, and there was a lot of underneath guys open, and so I was trying to get the ball to them and move the chains. It just kind of kept the offense going."

Mahomes said he didn't have any doubts entering the game about his right knee or ability to make the plays he needed to make in – and out – of the pocket.

"I trusted in those guys, the doctors and the training staff, when they told me I was ready to go," Mahomes said. "Obviously you want to get out there, get hit just to get yourself settled into the game. I had full confidence I was going to be able to play this game."

Mahomes said the rest even helped his left ankle, which he sprained in the season opener against Jacksonville and re-tweaked a few times in the following games.

"We knew we needed rest for the ankle, we knew we needed some days off," Mahomes said. "With having the knee, I got to rest that ankle and I was able to play and do what I could do, and I don't have any pain there."

Any doubts remaining about Mahomes' health disappeared in the fourth quarter. On a third-and-nine from the Kansas City 37-yard line, Mahomes stepped up in the pocket to avoid the rush and jumped in the air before absorbing a hit from linebacker Cameron Wake.

"I actually work a little bit with (quarterbacks) coach (Mike) Kafka and in the offseason on kind of throwing it and getting your hip through," Mahomes said of the jump pass. "That's another big part of how I get a lot of torque on my ball."

The gunslinger delivered a strike 20-yards down field to Mecole Hardman, who took the ball the rest of the way for a 63-yard touchdown that put the Chiefs up 29-20 with 12:04 to play in the game.

Tennessee running back Derrick Henry gashed the Chiefs in the Titans' win, rushing 23 times for 188 yards and two touchdowns.

"Mecole ran a great route, I had to throw it before he even broke, and he ran it exactly how I wanted him to, and that comes with repetition," Mahomes said. "Once you get the ball in those guys' hands, they can make plays happen."

Hardman didn't see Mahomes make the jump. He didn't even see the ball until it was in the air, but said it doesn't surprise him for Mahomes to make such as throw.

"That's Pat Mahomes," Hardman said. "I think that's all you got to say. He's Pat. That's what he does, he maneuvers in the pocket, he can get out of the pocket, he can make throws that people can't make."

Receiver Tyreek Hill, who caught a career-high 11 passes for 157 yards and a touchdown, came to a similar conclusion.

"That's just Pat being Pat, once again," Hill said. "He should have no-looked it. That would have been crazy."

Mahomes coming back and delivering another show-stopping performance after an ugly knee injury impressed Hill.

"It was amazing to see him out there having fun, playing the game he loves," Hill said. "It was amazing having him back out there." ∎

Chiefs 24, Chargers 17
November 18, 2019 • Mexico City, Mexico

Viva Mexico

Chiefs Defense Comes Up with Four Turnovers in South of the Border Win

It took a year longer than planned but the Chiefs finally stepped on the field at Estadio Azteca in Mexico City and the wait proved worth the while.

An opportunistic Kansas City defense came up with four turnovers against the Los Angeles Chargers, including interceptions on the final two drives of the game. The Chiefs offense wasn't always sharp, yet Kansas City still escaped with a 24-17 win.

Defensive end Frank Clark, who struggled dealing with a pinched nerve in his neck during much of the first half of the season, delivered his biggest game of the season with five tackles and seven total pressures against Philip Rivers, including a sack.

"I was real proud of our defense for the job that they did today," Reid said. "I think Frank Clark probably jumps out at you for the job that he did. He had a heck of a game. Four takeaways, the guys that intercepted the football, and then helped create the turnovers."

Clark seemed do play a role in every big play of the night, including the final defensive stop. The Chargers trailed by a touchdown but had the ball at the Kansas City 14-yard line with 24 seconds to go. With Clark bearing down in the pocket, Rivers forced a ball toward running back Austin Ekeler in the end zone. Safety Dan Sorensen read the play perfectly and picked off the pass for a touchback.

"I was proud of our defense, though, for closing the game out the way they did," Reid said. "And then Dan with the big interception at the end, that was a huge play.

Mahomes didn't have a stellar night through the air, completing 19-of-31 passing for 182 yards and touchdown with an interception. But he rushed for a career-high 59 yards. Most importantly to him he took a shot to his injured right knee with no ill effects.

"I was kind of sitting there like, man, that's the first time I've taken a shot there," Mahomes said. "I kind of just felt it and it felt fine and I got back up and kept going."

"There was times where you saw in the second half I kind of just took the check downs and hit the running backs out of the back field when I had those early in the game," Mahomes said. "Just going back and reevaluating myself during the game, during halftime, and realizing that if they're going to give depth and kind of take away our shots, we're going to have to take what's there and whenever we get the opportunities like with Kelce in the red zone there, you take advantage of those."

The Chiefs planned to visit Estadio Azteca last season to face the Los Angeles Rams. A concert and heavy rains damaged the field, however, and new sod laid down created conditions the NFL deemed unsafe. The game was moved to the Los Angeles Memorial Coliseum, where the Rams won 54-51.

Patrick Mahomes looks to pass during the first half in Mexico City.

Both teams seemed to have trouble finding their footing on the field at first, but Tyrann Mathieu didn't have any complaints.

"It wasn't that much of a factor," Mathieu said. "Maybe it was a little bit slick, but, I mean, we play in snow, we play in rain, we play in different conditions, so I don't think that necessarily was an issue for us.

The NFL and the Chiefs have worked to make inroads into the Mexico market, which made moving last year's game a disappointing blow. The Chiefs eagerly volunteered to go back to Mexico City for a road game, and Reid said the team received overwhelming hospitality.

"Phenomenal people." Reid said. "It was a great experience. I think the players would tell you the same thing. But I think what stands out to me are the people. They are just tremendous and so welcoming."

Mahomes found himself mesmerized by the building's history and the rabid NFL fans cheering during the game.

"To be a part of that is awesome," Mahomes said. "Something I'll be able to tell my kids, hopefully, later in life. And then the fans were amazing. They really were. They were cheering the whole game. It was loud. It was a great atmosphere." ■

Defensive back Rashad Fenton intercepts a pass intended for Chargers wide receiver Andre Patton.

Chiefs 40, Raiders 9
December 1, 2019 • Kansas City, Missouri

Getting Defensive

Red-Hot Chiefs Defense Fuels Big Win over Rival Raiders

The Raiders' visit to Arrowhead Stadium in Week 13 loomed as a compelling matchup between the top contenders in the AFC West, but it finished with the Chiefs proving their dominance inside the division once again in a 40-9 rout over Oakland.

The Chiefs have a five-game win streak against the Raiders and are winners of 10 of the last 11 between the two teams. Kansas City has won 25 of their last 27 games against AFC West opponents.

Usually when the Chiefs bury opponents, they do it behind a high-octane offense. But this time the defense and special teams provided the jump start. On Oakland's opening drive, Tyrann Mathieu picked off a Derek Carr pass to set the Chiefs up at the Oakland 47-yard line.

That was the first of three Oakland turnovers on the day, leading directly to 14 Kansas City points. The Chiefs defense generated just 12 turnovers in the team's first 10 games of the season. In the last two games against the Raiders and the Los Angeles Chargers, the Chiefs produced seven turnovers.

Left guard Andrew Wylie says the offense gets fired up when the defensive and special teams units make big plays.

"The defense plays great, started out with a pick, then got a pick-six, a fumble recovery," Wylie said. "When the defense shows up to play like that, it's not going to be close."

Patrick Mahomes concluded the team's opening 11-play drive with a 3-yard touchdown pass to Darrel Williams putting Kansas City ahead 7-0.

Mahomes extended the lead to 14-0 midway through the second quarter, scrambling 13 yards for a touchdown. Safety Juan Thornhill picked off a Carr pass on the Raiders' ensuing drive, putting Kansas City ahead 21-0 at the half.

The Chiefs eventually built a 31-0 lead thanks to a 50-yard field by Harrison Butker and a 3-yard touchdown run from LeSean McCoy. McCoy's touchdown run came after a booth review following an interception in the end zone by Raiders cornerback Trayvon Mullen. The replay official overturned the call on the field, ruling Mullen committed pass interference against Chiefs receiver Demarcus Robinson. That set up Kansas City with a first-and-goal at Raiders 3-yard line.

Raiders head coach Jon Gruden wasn't happy with the call.

"We had an interception that we felt we did intercept that was turned over by the Wizard of Oz or somebody," Gruden said. "I do not know what happened on that. That was a big play in the game, no doubt."

Oakland finally ended their scoring drought with a 34-yard Daniel Carlson field goal opening the fourth quarter, cutting the deficit to 31-3.

The Chiefs then worked on draining the clock, embarking on a 14-play, 75-yard drive consuming 9

Strong safety Tyrann Mathieu celebrates an interception in the first half, part of a shutdown performance by the Chiefs defense.

minutes and 32 seconds on the clock. Rookie running back Darwin Thompson ran the ball 11 times on the drive 44 yards, capped off with a 4-yard touchdown run for a 38-3 margin.

Center Austin Reiter said head coach Andy Reid issued a challenge to his offensive line before the drive.

"Coach Reid came over and told us basically, 'End this. Be physical, let's do it,'" Reiter said. "We stepped up to the challenge."

The Chiefs' offense mustered only 259 yards in the game. It's just the fourth time in franchise history the club scored 40 points or more while gaining fewer than 260 yards of offense. Reid said he saw enough good things to feel good about his offense despite the stats.

"Everything is not going to be perfect," Reid said. "You're dealing with some elements right now, you got to work through those things. There was enough good there that if we start critiquing a couple bad ones, then we're missing out on some pretty good ones."

Oakland finally broke into the end zone with 39 seconds remaining with Carr tossing a 4-yard touchdown pass to tight end Derek Carrier. But Chiefs defensive end Tanoh Kpassagnon blocked the kick on the point after touchdown try. Cornerback Charvarius Ward scooped up the ball and raced into the end zone for a rare defensive two-point conversion score.

According to Pro Football Reference, this is only the second game in NFL history to end with a 40-9 score. The Minnesota Vikings defeated the New Orleans Saints by that margin on Sept. 12, 1976. ∎

Defensive back Rashad Fenton (27) celebrates with teammates Darron Lee (50) and Byron Pringle (13) after forcing a fumble from the Oakland Raiders.

95

DEFENSIVE TACKLE

Chris Jones

Jones Loves to Play Football but His Commitment to Diet and Fitness Fueled His Stardom

Watching Chris Jones talk about his love for Cap'n Crunch milkshakes, fried chicken and the meatballs made by defensive coordinator Steve Spagnuolo's wife Maria, it's easy to think of him as the big, round kid from Mississippi who arrived in Kansas City in 2016.

But Jones has matured into much more than that for the Chiefs in the past few seasons, chiseling himself into a lean, muscular and savvy veteran who stands on the precipice of becoming one of the NFL's highest-paid defensive players.

Defensive line teammate Derrick Nnadi said he was shocked when he arrived as a rookie seeing how much preparation Jones puts into his trade and how that translates into success for himself and others in the team's front seven.

"He studies how other teams are going to attack him," Nnadi said. "Whether it's pass protection or run defense, he learns what they're going to do against him and then he decides to figure out how to counter that."

Jones learned as a rookie that if wanted to thrive as a professional he had to make changes, especially with his diet and fitness.

"Everything I did took effect at improving my game," Jones said. "How can I have more energy, how can I be more dominant on the field."

He tipped the scales at 315 pounds as a rookie – "Madden still got me at 315. I haven't been 315 in four years." He jettisoned pork from his diet, which meant saying goodbye to bacon. "I love breakfast food period," Jones said. He switched to a diet heavy on vegetables and fish.

Now Jones weighs in at 298. At the end of the season he adjusts his diet to shed a few more pounds, so by January he weighed 295. "I just like saying 298," he explained.

He still has his cheat days and superstitions. Last season he had a chicken sandwich before a game and had a sack, so he kept doing it. He would go to Chick-fil-a on Saturday, so he had a sandwich for the next day.

"I try to make sure I maintain my body weight and

Chris Jones consults with defensive coordinator Steve Spagnuolo during a home game against the Chargers.

body fat," Jones said. "It keeps me moving around, I feel faster, I don't feel as sluggish, especially without eating pork."

Chiefs head coach Andy Reid says he saw how the transformation paid off for Jones.

"You saw the change in his body and how he really took care of himself physically with diets and workouts and all of that this offseason," Reid said. "His body fat is way down. He works his fundamentals and techniques."

That hard work produced big results for Jones last season. He led the team with 15 1/2 sacks, including picking up at least one sack in an NFL-record 11-straight games.

Jones skipped the team's offseason program in hopes of a new contract. Some speculated Jones might continue his holdout into training camp, as others in similar situations have done, as a bargaining tool. But at the 2 p.m. deadline on July 26, Jones walked through the doors at Scanlon Hall on the campus of Missouri Western State University to join his teammates.

"No distractions, focus on winning the Super Bowl and a new defense," Jones said upon his arrival at camp. "I'm ready, I'm excited. I'm glad to be back and ready to work."

The Chiefs organization and his teammates understood; in the NFL everyone knows it's a business first, and players have to look out for themselves. Safety Tyrann Mathieu appreciated how Jones handled his contract situation.

"Most guys in that position, there's a lot of outside noise that dictates what they do," Mathieu said. "For him to be here, I think that just says a lot about his character, really who he is as a person. … A lot of respect for him, especially from our locker room just by him being here. He didn't have to come."

For the first time in his career, injuries slowed Jones in 2019. He played all 16 regular-season games his first three years in the league, but a core muscle injury kept him out for three games this season. He still managed to collect nine sacks and 63 total pressures in 13 games.

Injuries to other players left the Chiefs shorthanded at times, and the athleticism of Jones paid off again as the team used him to fill in as an edge rusher when not stationed inside at his usual tackle position.

Jones played 28 snaps in the AFC Championship game, gritting through a calf injury he suffered in practice two weeks earlier. He generated five pressures and picked up two tackles in the game. Jones said he wasn't worried playing with the injury.

"I knew if I went on the field, they were going to have to carry me off," he said.

During the celebration afterward Mathieu approached Jones and told him how much he appreciated him as a teammate.

"I know a lot of people may look at football players and see gladiators, as guys who fight through injuries and fight through other issues," Mathieu said. "I was more impressed with him and committing himself to us. It all brings me back to him showing up for training camp. He could've probably held out the entire camp, but I think that says a lot about him as a person, as a man."

Chris Jones sacks Patriots quarterback Tom Brady in a game the Chiefs went on to win 23-16.

Chiefs 23, Patriots 16
December 8, 2019 • Foxborough, Massachusetts

Breakthrough

Victory Over Patriots Shows Chiefs, Mahomes Can Win Big Games

Football players and coaches always talk about taking the season one game at time and never looking ahead, but no one takes that seriously in a matchup like the Chiefs faced in Week 14.

From the moment the Chiefs fell short in last year's AFC Championship game in overtime against New England, this was the game everyone in the organization circled. The Chiefs would only know if they were on a Super Bowl path if they could get past New England.

They did just that, with the defense holding Tom Brady to just 169 yards through the air and allowing just three points to the Patriots on three fourth-quarter possessions.

The Chiefs defense remained a work in progress much of the season, but now things seem moving in the right direction for Steve Spagnuolo's defensive squad. Frank Clark said this was a game the Chiefs wouldn't have won two months ago.

"We had to deal with the trials, deal with everything, and then you get past it and then you see the results," Clark said after a win that helped the Chiefs clinch a playoff berth and the AFC West title. "That's kind of what we're seeing now. You're seeing the results of all the stuff we had to go through back then."

The win didn't come without some pain, however. Patrick Mahomes suffered a bruised right hand but it didn't stop him from finishing 26-of-40 passing for 283 yards and a touchdown. His lone interception came on the drive before the injury.

"It doesn't feel great right now," Mahomes said after the game. "It's something that you play with. In this sport you're going to get hurt, you're going to bang something, and so for me it's about going out there and competing and relying on my teammates to help me out whenever I'm not feeling maybe 100 percent."

The injury occurred on the first play of the team's second offensive drive in the first quarter. Mahomes attempted to scramble out of the pocket before dumping off a pass at the feet of running back LeSean McCoy. Patriots linebacker John Simon brought Mahomes to the ground as he released the ball, and the quarterback landed awkwardly on his right hand.

"I knew something was wrong, but I didn't know for sure," said Mahomes, who could be see holding and shaking his hand much of the game. "Then I tried to fire the next pass and it didn't look too pretty, so I kind of just let the trainers look at it."

After leading the Chiefs on nine-play, 53-yard drive culminating in a 48-yard field goal by Harrison Butker, Mahomes went to the sidelines for an evaluation. After a few warmup throws on the sideline, athletic trainers cleared Mahomes to return to the game.

The injury kept Mahomes from gripping the ball as he normally does, causing the Chiefs to streamline the game plan with more short throws.

"(The trainers) gave me the good-to-go," Mahomes said, "and so I went out there, battled, figured out ways

Tight end Travis Kelce fights for more yards after catching a pass in the first half.

to throw the ball across the middle and maybe not shoot those long shots that I usually throw but enough to get them back and still score touchdowns."

The game appeared in jeopardy for the Chiefs even before it began. A container of the team's equipment was not unloaded by the airline upon the club's arrival at the airport Saturday afternoon. The Chiefs' equipment managers couldn't setup Saturday due to state high school championship games held at Gillette Stadium. The crew arrived early Sunday morning and immediately discovered the missing gear of helmets, shoulder pads and other equipment.

Once the container was tracked down, the club arranged transportation for the trip to the stadium. Thanks to an escort provided by the Massachusetts State Police, equipment managers began unloading the gear at 2:49 p.m. eastern time for the 4:25 p.m. kickoff.

Reid says never worried the equipment wouldn't show up for the game.

"I think everybody did a good job getting it back here," Reid said. "We had plenty of time, and we rolled."

If the equipment didn't arrive, the Chiefs likely would have faced a forfeit.

"We might have had to share helmets if it didn't get here," quarterback Patrick Mahomes said.

It did not appear that all of the team's players took part in early pregame warmup, but a club employee did not expect any issues for full team pregame warmups that take place before kickoff. Spotted among the bags brought into the stadium was the equipment belonging to Mahomes.

"I had to warm up in some different stuff than I played in," Mahomes said. "But it was here in time for me to be able to go out to the real warm-ups. So just going out there – I mean, they always keep extra stuff around so they took care of us and found a way to make it work and we just kept rolling."

Reid said everyone stayed calm including players and coaches as well as the team's equipment managers.

"It happens," Reid said. "It wasn't a big deal. I've been doing it for a lot of years and one out of how many years I've been doing it, it keeps things exciting." ∎

Despite dealing with a bruised right hand, Patrick Mahomes finished 26-of-40 passing for 283 yards.

Rebuilding the Defense

How a Head Coach, a General Manager and a Coordinator Built a Championship Defense

The 2018 Chiefs defense couldn't have sunk much lower. The club ranked 31st in the league in allowing 405.5 yards per game and 31st in pass defense yielding 273.4 yards per game. The run defense was marginally better, ranking 27th in allowing 132.1 per game.

All the meanwhile the Chiefs had the league's No. 1 offense in terms of total yards and points. Something had to give. Eventually it did when head coach Andy Reid decided to part ways with defensive coordinator Bob Sutton. It wasn't an easy decision, despite the numbers.

"I love Bob Sutton, Bob and I talk, we're still friends," Reid said a month after the decision. "Sometimes that's this business. Sometimes change can be good for both sides."

When Reid first took over as head coach in Philadelphia, one of his first hires was bringing on board Steve Spagnuolo as a defensive assistant, but their friendship extends back to their days on college sidelines. Now he turned to his old friend as defensive coordinator.

"He kind of knows how I roll with offense, and I know how he rolls with defense," Reid said.

Reid banked on the comfort level between himself and Spagnuolo playing an important role in the Chiefs developing a defensive style that complements its high-octane offense.

"I think the end result needs to be complementary where both sides play well, and that's the best thing," Reid said. "He's going to strive. He's not striving for, 'OK, we're going to be in the midpoint of the league on defense.' He's striving to be the best he possibly can on the defensive side."

Spagnuolo spent the 2018 season off the sidelines but not exactly out of football. After being bypassed by the New York Giants to remain on board after serving as interim head coach, he went back home to Philadelphia. He took time to relax and decompress. He would travel to Mt. Laurel, New Jersey each week to the headquarters for NFL Films to watch tapes of teams from across the league.

"The challenge was missing football and the camaraderie of coaches, players," Spagnuolo said. "Not being at training camp where it's nice and hot and you are doing football that was a challenge, I was missing it. The rewards were sitting back and seeing a big picture view of the NFL and the game of football, as opposed to being in these buildings during the season and having the blinders on to the team you are about to play."

Spagnuolo return to the sidelines full of energy and loaded with "oodles of notes" for plays to pull. But before he could put his team on the field, however, it was up to general manager Brett Veach to put together a roster for him. The first steps: purging the roster of veterans Justin Houston, Eric Berry and Dee Ford.

Could those players help the Chiefs win in 2019?

After early growing pains in the first half of the season, the Chiefs defense under Steve Spagnuolo sharpened for the final stretch.

Certainly, Veach said, but when balancing draft capital and salary cap space, the question is for how long they can help the team win.

"You've got to take that into consideration," Veach said. "You look at can they help us at the cost of what it would take to do that, again knowing that contracts and extensions are looming behind here. What can we do now to put ourselves in a good position not just for next year, but again for the next three, four, five, six years?"

With a defensive roster now purged of most of its star power and veteran leadership, Veach scoured the free agent pool and the trade markets for potential replacements. He walked into Spagnuolo's office and gave him a list of safeties to watch on tape and grade. One of the names was Tyrann Mathieu.

"He would go down the list," Veach said, "and he would say strengths and weaknesses and, 'I like this guy,' this and that, 'here's what he can do, here's what he can't do.' He got to (Mathieu) and he said, 'I'm struggling to find what he can't do.' I said, 'Say no more, we're going to get him.'"

The Chiefs also had to augment their rushing attack, and one name stood out: Seattle defensive end Frank Clark. The Chiefs made a trade for Clark and locked him up with a new long-term contract. Veach also added defensive ends Alex Okafor and Emmanuel Ogbah, linebackers Damien Wilson and Darron Lee and cornerback Bashaud Breeland.

"We believed in the guys we went after," Veach said. "We knew that we had to field a defense to complement our offense and we did that."

During the offseason program, Spagnuolo played the role of mad scientist, tinkering with lineups and rotations. That continued into the regular season. He thought it might take the first month of the season before the defense started showing its true colors.

But after 10 weeks the results were mixed. The Chiefs stood 6-4 and their run defense ranked 30th in the league allowing 143.1 yards per game. The pass defense improved to 14th but the ranked 19th in allowing 23.3 points per game.

"I think the scheme works," Spagnuolo said. "I think we play in a scheme were all 11 guys have to believe in the play call. We can continue to get better with that. I think things will take care of themselves."

Spagnuolo always had faith his defense would click but it took longer than expected. He did the only thing he could do at midseason – he continued having faith.

"You can't live tackle (in practice), we're not in pads, the whole thing," Spagnuolo said. "But for what it is we can do, they're doing it and more. They care about it. I can work with guys like that. They care, they're passionate, they hurt as much as anybody, they want to get it fixed. Sometimes it takes a little while."

Over the final six weeks of the season, the Chiefs fielded arguably the best defense in the league. They ranked No. 1 in scoring, No. 5 in rushing yards allowed and No. 13 in pass defense.

It's said success has many friends while failure is an orphan. Had the Chiefs defense failed in its mission in 2019, Spagnuolo might likely have taken the blame. Reid sees plenty of reason to spread recognition around.

"(Spagnuolo) didn't have to teach the coaches," Reid said. "The coaches just hit the ground running and already knew what was expected of them. Therefore, the players go, 'Man, all of these guys believe this, they can teach it, they're all tied in.' With that, there was a confidence that was built in. Even when things start off slow, the guys are going, 'We're this close, we're this close to turning this thing around again to the way we want it.' They just kept at it and kept at it." ■

Strong safety Tyrann Mathieu celebrates during the Chiefs' Week 16 win against the Bears.

Chiefs 23, Broncos 3
December 15, 2019 • Kansas City, Missouri

Whiteout

Chiefs Bury Broncos in Snowy Arrowhead Stadium

Patrick Mahomes showed no ill effects from the bruised right hand he suffered the week before in New England, passing for more than 300 yards with help from tight end Travis Kelce as the Chiefs cruised past the Broncos 23-3 in a snowstorm at Arrowhead Stadium.

"I think I'm a snow-game guy," Mahomes said while mic'd up during the game. "I don't know why but I kind of like it. Everything is super slow and I'm just like out here just standing straight in the pocket like 'whoop.'"

Reid said the conditions nor the injury affected his quarterback Sunday.

"I thought he threw it around real well and spun it," Reid said. "I thought all in all he had a great day. It was a pretty phenomenal day."

Mahomes finished the game 27-of-34 passing for 340 yards, two touchdowns and an interception. Kelce became the first tight end in league history to collect more than 1,000 yards receiving in four-straight seasons. The Broncos never found a solution for breaking up the Mahomes-Kelce duo, with the tight end hauling in 11 catches on 13 targets for 141 yards.

The Chiefs jumped out to an early lead when Mahomes connected with Tyreek Hill on a 41-yard post route for a touchdown on their first drive of the game. A botched snap in the driving snowstorm left the Chiefs on top 6-0.

Hill said the ability Mahomes possesses to throw the ball anywhere in the field combined with his own improved route running makes that touchdown play possible.

"Obviously we practiced it during the week, it's just the connection and the bond me and Patrick got," Hill said. "Not only me, but all of the receivers. I feel like anyone one of us could have made that play.

Kansas City built a 12-0 leading on two Harrison Butker field goals from 23 and 24 yards before the Broncos got on the board. Kicker Brandon McManus connected on a 32-yard field with 1:56 remaining in the second quarter.

The Chiefs responded with a quick scoring drive of their own before the end of the half. Butker hit from 44 yards out as time expired, putting Kansas City up 15-3 at the break. Butker now has 411 points scored through the first three seasons of his NFL career, eclipsing the previous best of 409 points set by New Orleans Saints kicker Will Lutz to start a career.

Butker said he wore a seven-stud cleat on his left plant foot to guard against slipping in the snow, but wore a soccer cleat on his right kicking leg. The cleat doesn't allow the kicker to generate as much power, which

Travis Kelce is brought down by Broncos inside linebacker Todd Davis.

requires a bit of an adjustment.

"It is a challenge, but it's something that you got to overcome," Butker said. "As an NFL kicker, it doesn't matter what the situation is, the ball's got to go through the uprights."

Mahomes opened the second half leading his team on a 75-yard, 5 minute, 15 second drive capped off with a 5-yard touchdown pass to Hill. Hill caught five passes for 67 yards and two scores in the contest.

The win over the Broncos snapped a two-game winning streak for Denver's rookie quarterback Drew Lock. The native of Lee's Summit, Missouri, struggled in his first career game against the team he cheered for as a youth, completing 18-of-40 passes for 208 yards and an interception.

Lock said he's disappointed in the loss, but he enjoyed what he hopes serves as the first of many visits to his hometown as a starting NFL quarterback.

"Having the chance to play here was awesome," Lock said. "Obviously you would like to win, but I don't think this is the last time I will be visiting Arrowhead. I would like to think that it will be like this every time we come here and play in Arrowhead."

Kansas City lost two starters to injury during the game. Defensive end Alex Okafor left with a pectoral injury after collecting a sack against Lock in the first half and did not return. Left guard Andrew Wylie left late in the fourth quarter with a sprained left ankle, creating an opening for veteran Stefen Wisniewski. ◼

Running back Spencer Ware (39) fights his way through the Denver Broncos defense.

87

TIGHT END

Travis Kelce

Despite Big Numbers, Kelce Still Overlooked as a Potential Future Hall of Fame Tight End

While he plays with plenty of style and flair, it sometimes seems Chiefs tight end Travis Kelce entered the ranks of the NFL's best tight ends quietly. While the likes of Rob Gronkowski and now San Francisco's George Kittle grab accolades, Kelce continues grabbing catches and gobbling up yards at a record pace.

The seventh-year pro made history in Week 11 when he became the fastest tight end in league history with 450 catches and 6,000 yards in a career. He performed the feat in 91 career games, three games faster than Hall of Fame member Kellen Winslow and seven games faster than retired Patriots tight end Rob Gronkowski.

In Week 15 against the Broncos Kelce eclipsed the 1,000-yard mark for the fourth straight season, the longest streak in league history for a tight end. He previously shared the mark with Carolina Panthers tight end Greg Olsen, who posted three-straight 1,000-yard seasons from 2014 to 2016.

In Week 16 in Chicago, Kelce reached 500 receptions in 95 career games, six games faster than the previous best by a tight end, also by Winslow. Additionally, he reached 1,200 yards receiving on the season in that game, making him the first tight end in league history to do that in back-to-back seasons.

Yet quarterback Patrick Mahomes says there's more to Kelce's importance to the Chiefs offense than his statistics.

"I think the biggest thing with Travis is he does all these things but the type of person he is, is the greatest thing he can do," Mahomes said. "He's able to try to help everyone else out to get open and when his number is called, he just makes the play and does whatever he can to move the chains or score the touchdown and help the team."

Despite the rocket-like trajectory of his career, Kelce says he struggled making the transition to the NFL in his rookie season in 2013. A knee injury limited him to one game, and he didn't truly understand what it meant to be a pro. Just as Alex Smith later mentored Mahomes as a rookie, Kelce had his own veteran who showed him the ropes.

"I struggled with the playbook originally," Kelce said. "On top of that, mentally I don't think I was quite there as a professional. I got to see a guy like Anthony Fasano, a true pro's pro, how he came into work every single day, how he attacked the games, how he talked about the

2019 marked Travis Kelce's fourth straight season with over 1,000 receiving yards.

game. That helped me out tremendously and really took my career to another level."

Kelce also says he benefits from playing for Andy Reid.

"I've been fortunate to be with Andy Reid my entire career," Kelce said. "To be able to be in his system over a substantial amount of time, you kind of get into the play callers' mind and how he wants certain routes ran versus certain defenses and you just find what's comfortable. I'm just a product of Andy Reid."

Reid encourages his players to let their personalities come through in their play, and sometimes that means the best and the worst for Kelce. During the Chiefs 19-13 loss to the Indianapolis Colts in Week 6, a flash of the emotional Kelce showed up. After a rough start to the game, he snapped at offensive coordinator Eric Bieniemy on the sideline.

"It's something that immediately I regretted, and I just wanted to make it good and let him know that I'm ready to rock 'n' roll for you," Kelce said.

Television cameras caught Kelce and Bieniemy on the sidelines in a conversation, which ended with Kelce appearing to shove the coach. Cameras also caught the two shortly afterward patching things up between them.

"You guys saw me hug him afterward," Kelce said. "I love that guy, and that will never change, and I appreciate him always being on my tail to get me going."

Kelce feels he and Bieniemy are wired the same way when it comes to their competitive nature. He described Bieniemy as a father figure.

"I love him, he's helped me out tremendously as a person, as a professional and I'm sure he'll keep doing that throughout the rest of my career," Kelce said. "And just what happened on the sidelines, sometimes football you get a little heated with your brothers or your coaches."

Bieniemy agreed.

"Trav is one of the top players that I've been fortunate and blessed to coach," Bieniemy said. "But also too, he's a very passionate individual, and so am I."

This season also saw how the emotional side can bring out the best in others around him. Kelce stole the show after the AFC Championship game when he grabbed the microphone from CBS' Jim Nantz and screamed, "You've gotta fight for your right to party" to the faithful at Arrowhead Stadium.

"It's something I knew could get the crowd riled up and get them involved," Kelce said. "That's going to be something I remember for the rest of my life."

Despite the accolades, Kelce still seems a bit overlooked on the national stage. Playing in the biggest game could go a long way in cementing his status as the league's top tight end.

"Travis has played a lot of great football in his career and I know he's super excited to play in the Super Bowl and get a chance to play for it," Mahomes said.

Kelce says he wants to finish his career in Kansas City. He feels a connection to the fans, and even though he only joined the club in 2013, he feels the same half-century of frustration that Chiefs fans felt before returning to the Super Bowl.

"It seems like I've been here the entire 50 years that we haven't found our way back to the Super Bowl," Kelce said. "Just my seven years alone have felt like an eternity, so I can only imagine what this would mean to the community if we bring this thing back."

Chiefs head coach Andy Reid said he believes the 30-yard-old Kelce still has some of his best football ahead of him.

"He wants to get better," Reid said. "That's probably more important than the ability to get better. He wants to get better in all areas of his game which makes it enjoyable to coach the guy. You see him grow over the years as a player and a teammate and all those things. He's got great ability. He knows how to play the game. He's another one of those guys that has a good feel for it." ■

Travis Kelce celebrates a touchdown against the Packers in Week 8.

Chiefs 26, Bears 3
December 22, 2019 • Chicago, Illinois

Suggs Comes to KC

Chiefs Keep Win Streak Going with Key Defensive Addition

The Chiefs' defense continued its late season surge, holding the Chicago Bears to just 234 yards of offense in a 26-3 win at Soldier Field on Sunday Night Football, but it was the newest member of the Chiefs defense attracting the most attention.

Six days earlier, the Chiefs opened an early Christmas present, claiming defensive end Terrell Suggs off waivers from the Arizona Cardinals. The addition of Suggs came less than 24 hours after the Chiefs placed Alex Okafor on season-ending injured reserve.

Initial reports said that after 17 seasons in the NFL, Suggs wouldn't report to any team claiming him other than the Baltimore Ravens, the club where Suggs spent 16 of those seasons and won a Super Bowl ring. But after discussions with general manager Brett Veach, defensive coordinator Steve Spagnuolo and most importantly Andy Reid, Suggs bought in to joining the Chiefs.

"I asked coach, I just learned the hard way that a player like me doesn't just fit in anywhere," Suggs explained. "Coach Reid said, 'Trust me, you'll fit in here.' I took him at his word, and it's been pretty exciting, been pretty fun since I got here."

The box score shows just one assisted tackle for Suggs in his first game with the Chiefs, but that doesn't tell the whole story. Chicago's first drive came to a halt when Suggs roared past Bears left tackle Charles Leno and chased quarterback Mitchell Trubisky out of the pocket.

Suggs couldn't corral Trubisky, but his defensive end companion Frank Clark cleaned up with an 8-yard sack, forcing the Bears to punt.

Reid said after the game that it's great to see Suggs join the club. The coach thought the veteran delivered a nice performance his first time out with his new team.

"The first couple of times he was in he got pressures on the quarterback," Reid said. "That's a nice mix for a guy that's probably a future Hall of Famer here. We're excited to have him on board."

Safety Tyrann Mathieu said Suggs immediately proved a great addition.

"There's a lot of experience that he brings," Mathieu said. "He's going to help out Frank and Chris (Jones) and all those guys a lot. I think it's a perfect time to add a guy like that the team."

Suggs in less than a week quickly bought in to what the Chiefs are doing defensively.

"At the end of the day it's just football," Suggs said. "But it is really exciting to kind of join this team. The swagger that they're playing with and the confidence and the energy, that felt really good."

His Chiefs teammates appeared in a bit of awe of their new teammate. Clark wears No. 55 partly in tribute to Suggs and other NFL players he watched growing up. Clark's defensive coordinator and position coach at Michigan, Greg Mattison, also coached Suggs in Baltimore.

Outside linebacker Terrell Suggs runs around the edge as Chicago Bears offensive tackle Charles Leno blocks.

"Coach Mattison, he gave me the game on T-Suggs and I've been watching film on him since college," Clark said. "It kind of helped me develop some of the things I do in my game. Since he's been here just been thankful and just happy to have a player in our locker room, and specifically in our room, of his caliber."

Suggs finds himself joining a defense on a red-hot streak.

The Chiefs have held opponents to just 9.6 points per game during the club's five-game winning streak. They stand 11-4 heading into next week's season finale against the Los Angeles Chargers.

Mathieu thinks the defense is peaking at just the right time after dealing with adversity through the first half of the season.

"I think we know who we are defensively," Mathieu said. "I think we know that we have the guys to get it done. We have been really committing ourselves to preparing the right way."

Suggs says he wants to get more involved after a successful six days with Kansas City.

"It's been overwhelming," Suggs said. "It's been very flattering, like I said. I'm very honored to join this team in their role. I'm glad to be a part of it."

On the other side of the ball, the Chiefs' offense did its part as well. Mahomes completed 23-of-33 passing for 240 yards and two touchdowns. He also scrambled for a 12-yard touchdown.

On his second pass of the game, Mahomes connected with wide receiver Sammy Watkins for a 17-yard gain. That put him over the 9,000-yard mark for his career, reaching that milestone in just his 30th career game. Kurt Warner previously owned that distinction, reaching that level in 32 games. Mahomes now has 9,227 passing yards in his career.

His two touchdown passes also made Mahomes the fastest quarterback to reach 75 career touchdown throws. Dan Marino reached that mark in 31 games. ■

Terrell Suggs immediately stepped up for the Chiefs in his first game after being claimed off waivers from the Cardinals.

Chiefs 31, Chargers 21

December 29, 2019 • Kansas City, Missouri

Top Dog Thanks to Underdog

Chiefs claim No. 2 seed with help from Dolphins

The Chiefs entered the final week of the season in a precarious situation. The club held the No. 3 position in the AFC playoff seedings. Remaining in that position meant hosting a Wild Card playoff game against the No. 6, at that moment the Tennessee Titans.

A loss to the Los Angeles Chargers coupled with a win by the Houston Texans and the Chiefs could fall to the No. 4 seed, leaving them to face the Buffalo Bills in the Wild Card round at Arrowhead Stadium.

There was a third far less likely possibility. With a Kansas City win and a New England loss at home to the Miami Dolphins, the Chiefs would claim the No. 2 seed, which would mean a bye in the first round followed by a home playoff game.

Only one problem with that scenario; the Patriots entered the game as 16-point favorites against the 4-11 Dolphins.

The Chargers meanwhile had given the Chiefs their own troubles of late despite Kansas City winning 10 of the last 11 games between the two clubs. The Chargers beat the Chiefs in Arrowhead in December 2018, and only a late interception sealed Kansas City's win in Mexico City earlier this season.

Chargers quarterback Philip Rivers connected with Keenan Allen for a 12-yard touchdown in the second quarter to give Los Angeles a 7-3 second-quarter lead. Patrick Mahomes and Demarcus Robinson teamed up for a 24-yard touchdown that put the Chiefs ahead 10-7 at halftime.

On the opening drive of the second half, Chargers cornerback Michael Davis intercepted a Mahomes pass, setting up Los Angeles at the Kansas City 21-yard line. Three plays later Melvin Gordon went into the end zone from 5 yards out and the Chargers led 14-10.

All season long the Chiefs return team felt it was close to breaking a big play, and it finally happened. Rookie returner Mecole Hardman took the ball from 4 yards deep in the end zone, found a crease and a raced down the sideline 104 yards for a touchdown, immediately flipping the momentum of the game.

Hardman said special teams coach Dave Toub gave him the green light to bring the ball out of the end zone if he saw an opportunity.

"If you want to take it out, you just be smart with it," Hardman said. "At the end of the day, it's kind of up to me. But he trusts me with whatever I want to do, and today I felt it."

Chris Jones led the celebrations after the Chiefs learned they had clinched the No. 2 seed.

Later in the third quarter running back Damien Williams broke a couple of tackles in racing 84 yards for a touchdown that proved the game winner. He credited left tackle Eric Fisher for creating the opportunity for him to break off the long run.

"I saw Fish do a great job kicking the guy out so all I had to do was hit the hole as hard as I could, which is why I was breaking all those tackles," Williams said. "I trusted my O-line to hit it with velocity."

Williams, in his second game since returning from a rib injury, picked up 124 yards on the ground along with two touchdowns on just 12 carries. He also added 30 yards receiving on four catches.

The Chiefs carried a 24-14 lead into the fourth quarter, but the players on the field had no idea what was happening in New England. Head coach Andy Reid wanted to keep his team's focus on the task at hand rather than worry about the Patriots and Dolphins.

"Even if that game didn't go right, we still needed to play for the game that's happening this afternoon," Reid said. "We wouldn't have an idea. We didn't care."

The Chiefs had no idea the Patriots and Dolphins were tied entering the fourth quarter. Just as Chargers tight end Hunter Henry hauled in an 8-yard pass from Rivers to pull within 24-21 with 5:23 remaining, Tom Brady connected with James White for a 13-yard score to put the Patriots ahead 24-20 with 3:53 remaining.

Williams scored his second touchdown of the day with 2:37 remaining in the game. At that moment, the Dolphins set up for a first-and-goal from the 5-yard line. With CBS broadcaster Kevin Harlan calling both games at once, Miami quarterback Ryan Fitzpatrick found tight end Mike Gesicki for a touchdown putting the Dolphins ahead 27-24 with 29 second remaining.

Word shortly filtered to the players on the field, including defensive end Terrell Suggs.

"Then it hit us, 'Oh my God, really?'" Suggs said. "It's very flattering, but it shows good stuff can happen when you handle your own business. You focus on what you have to do, your task at hand. You can't worry about anybody else."

Mahomes found out the result when fans erupted for no apparent reason.

"It's basically like winning a playoff game and then getting to play a game at home," Mahomes said. "We're excited for that and we're going to keep building and keep trying to build this momentum and keep it going."

Reid joked after the game about sending Fitzpatrick some Kansas City Steaks. "I can't do that though because that's tampering, so I'm not going to do that. But he deserves them."

The outcome proved Reid prescient for wanting to keep his team in the dark about anything other than the task at hand.

"It's not easy because you don't know the scores and you have to have mindset coming into this thing," Reid said. "The Dolphins were a 16-point underdog going into this. It's a great example of why you play. If you're on that field, you go 100 miles per hour and you play your heart out." ∎

Damien Williams runs for his second touchdown of the day during the second half.

Championship Swagger

Veteran Newcomers Tyrann Mathieu and Frank Clark
Create New Culture on Defense

Frank Clark rarely hides his emotions, usually carrying a broad smile on his face and ready for a quick quip. Unless he's on the field facing off against an offensive tackle.

"I don't really get emotional out there," Clark said with a laugh. "It's this man, this guy that comes over me sometimes on Sundays when I'm on the field. It's no choice, I've got to go to that place to help my teammates out the best I can."

That's the attitude the Chiefs were seeking when they traded for Clark in the offseason and made him the highest-paid player in franchise history with a new contract. When Clark took a seat on the stage inside the Hank Stram Theatre at the Chiefs' training complex for his introductory press conference the first question asked concerned what he brought to a defense seeking a new identity.

"I feel like I bring a type of attitude and swagger with my play that I feel like every coach loves and I feel like my teammates will love," Clark said. "I feel like it's infectious."

Just a few weeks later the Chiefs hit the practice field for their offseason program, and newly arrived safety Tyrann Mathieu echoed Clark's remarks when asked to explain what he, Clark and their teammates were hoping to accomplish.

"It's really trying to build a defense with an attitude," Mathieu said. "I think any time you can have 10 or 11 guys with a chip on their shoulder, with an edge,

a certain kind of presence, a certain kind of attitude, a certain kind of swagger you can create a collective identity and I think that's really what we're trying to do. "

Not long after that, Mathieu officially introduced his teammates on defense to what would become their mantra – "championship swagger."

To Mathieu, championship swagger is more than a phrase; it's a way of life on the football field for players who want to win. It's the "idea of where you want to go and everything that it takes to get there." The patron saint of championship swagger is Hall of Fame cornerback Deion Sanders, who exuded confidence and style while earning nine All-Pro honors in the 1990s and winning back-to-back Super Bowls playing for San Francisco and Dallas.

"I think body language is really important, which we do a great job with," Mathieu said. "I think your commitment to the process is extremely important. Then, the film study and being prepared so that when you do go out there on Sunday, everybody knows that you know what's going on. Like Deion used to say, 'when you look good, you play good.'"

No one embodies championship swagger more than Mathieu. At the team's kickoff luncheon in August, he said it was an everyday challenge for the team to create a new culture and fulfill the vision set out by head coach Andy Reid and general manager Brett Veach.

"Most of us are new, it's a new system, new scheme,

Newcomer Tyrann Mathieu cultivated "championship swagger" all season among his Chiefs teammates.

new coaches, new personalities that we have to adjust to," he said. "But I think defensively, if you can have a group of guys with a certain identity, swagger, attitude, how they approach each and every day, whether or not they're willing to die on their feet, I think that's the kind of guys that you want to play defense with, and that's the kind of group we want to have.

When he learned the Chiefs fans refer themselves as Chiefs Kingdom, Mathieu thought of the word "landlord." Three days before the season opener, Mathieu tweeted out an image of himself with just the words "KINGDOM LANDLORDS."

It wasn't long before teammates started calling Mathieu "Landlord," an identify he played into immediately, proclaiming to collect "rent" from opponents after each victory.

"I think ultimately, they brought me here to kind of be that guy, right?" Mathieu told Yahoo Sports. "Obviously, you don't really like to rush nicknames … but I just felt like that was my position, that was the title Veach gave me during the first conversation we had. He didn't say 'Landlord,' but he made me feel like hey, this is gonna be my ship to run, and that's kinda where that comes from."

Even the offense – which doesn't necessarily need a boost of confidence – started buying into playing with attitude, as tight end Travis Kelce described the competitive nature of quarterback Patrick Mahomes.

"I think that has a lot to do with this team and how much energy this team has, the chemistry, the swagger, whatever you want to call it," Kelce said. "There is a lot of fun in this locker room and it is because of the guys that are in this locker room."

The addition of defensive end Terrell Suggs brought championship swagger to another level, Mathieu said. Suggs, whose nickname "T-Sizzle" has plenty of swag on its own, brought 17 years of experience to Kansas City along with a Super Bowl ring he won in Baltimore.

"He's a true veteran," Mathieu said of Suggs. "I think he has a lot of that championship swagger. He comes to work every day. Always taking notes. I can remember a few plays in the game where he was scrapping down the ball and he looks like he's 28."

Suggs said he saw the attitude of the defense the moment he joined the club in December.

"This team plays with tremendous swag," Suggs said. "It's a confidence. That's the number one edge that a football player has – confidence. When you have a team that's playing with swagger, and the head ball coach is encouraging that and your position coach is encouraging that, that can help you in January in playoff football."

Defensive coordinator Steve Spagnuolo doesn't have a definition for "championship swagger – "I don't even know what a swagger is to be honest with you" – but he is sure about one thing regarding his defense and Mathieu.

"They have it," he said. "He has it. Most of them do. To me, it is a confidence thing. You can't play this game or be successful in this particular game unless you are confident. You have to believe in yourself. You have to be secure in yourself.

"I don't know if that is his definition, but that's what I can see." ■

Frank Clark channels championship swagger during the AFC Championship game against the Titans.

Chiefs 51, Texans 31
January 12, 2020 • Kansas City, Missouri

Comeback Kids

Chiefs Rally from 24-0 Deficit in Routing Texans

The Chiefs could do very little right for the first 20 minutes of their Divisional Round playoff game against Houston, but they did very little wrong afterward, scoring touchdowns on seven straight possessions in rallying from a 24-0 deficit to a 51-31 rout over the Texans.

"When you're down 24-0 and you don't have a good locker room, things can go the wrong way for you," head coach Andy Reid said afterward. "The guys all hung together."

The victory sent the Chiefs to the AFC Championship Game at home for the second year in a row. That 37-31 overtime loss to New England set everything in motion for this season that left the Chiefs wanting for more.

But hosting their second-straight AFC title game at Arrowhead Stadium seemed a remote possibility against Houston as the Chiefs fell behind 24-0 early in the second quarter.

Texans quarterback Deshaun Watson got his team off to a quick start on the game's first series with a 54-yard touchdown pass to Kenny Stills on a busted coverage, leaving him wide open in the second secondary.

The Texans quickly expanded their lead on Kansas City's first possession. Lonnie Johnson Jr. recovered a punt blocked by Barkevious Mingo for a 10-yard touchdown return. Watson led the Texans on another touchdown drive in the first quarter, capped off with a 4-yard touchdown pass to Darren Fells.

Yet the situation on the sideline never got out of control, said right tackle Mitchell Schwartz. Eventually, the offense began executing.

"I think it just shows the determination of the team," Schwartz said. "If we had any doubts or waiver ideas, I don't think we would have come back."

After Ka'imi Fairbairn expanded the Texans' lead to 24-0 with a 31-yard field, Reid had a simple message for his team.

"I just said, 'This isn't you, just get back, relax,'" Reid said. "'Pump the breaks here for a second, refocus and let's go.' It's that simple really."

Meanwhile Mahomes patrolled the sideline with a message for all of his teammates: "Let's go do something special."

"Everybody is already counting us out," he said. "Let's just go play by play and put our best effort out there. I knew that as a team everything had to go the right way."

The Chiefs needed a break at that point, and they got it from rookie returner Mecole Hardman. The Pro Bowler broke off a 58-yard return on the ensuing kickoff, and he immediately felt the momentum shifting in his team's direction.

"After that I could see it," Hardman said. "Everything went crazy. The crowd got into it, and when the crowd gets into it it's a hostile environment to play in. I felt like we could do no wrong."

Patrick Mahomes scrambles during the second half against the Texans.

Two plays later Patrick Mahomes connected with running back Damien Williams for a 17-yard touchdown to end the scoring drought. Now it was the Texans' turn to make a costly mistake.

The Chiefs held Houston to a three and out on their next possession, but Texans head coach Bill O'Brien took a gamble. Facing a fourth-and-4 from their own 31-yard line, safety Justin Reid took a direct snap from the punt formation for a fake. Kansas City safety Dan Sorensen sniffed it out, however.

"When I saw him take that snap outside, I just closed in, made the tackle," Sorensen said.

Three plays later Mahomes found tight end Travis Kelce for a five-yard touchdown pass to cut the lead to 24-14. Sorensen made another huge play on the ensuing kickoff, knocking the ball out of the hands of returner DeAndre Carter. Rookie Darwin Thompson caught the loose ball on the fly and returned it to the Houston six-yard line. Three plays later, Mahomes and Kelce connected again for a six-yard touchdown catch, cutting the edge to 24-21.

Mahomes and Kelce weren't done, hooking up for another 5-yard touchdown catch with 44 seconds remaining in the half. Kansas City scored 28 points in the last 10 minutes of the second quarter, taking a 28-24 lead at the break.

"I thought the defense stepped up," Mahomes said. "The special teams stepped up. Offensively we started making the plays we weren't making and play-by-play we just chipped away at that lead. Then we go to the half and then in the second half we kept firing."

Indeed, the rout continued in the second half, with Williams rushing for two touchdowns and the Chiefs reaching the end zone on an NFL postseason record seven straight possessions.

Running back Damien Williams (26) scores a touchdown past Houston Texans safety Justin Reid (20) to kick off the incredible comeback effort.

Mahomes finished the game 23-of-35 passing for 321 yards and five touchdowns. Kelce caught a career-best three touchdown passes while leading the Chiefs with 10 catches for 134 yards.

The win puts the Chiefs one victory from capturing the Lamar Hunt Trophy in the 50th anniversary season of the team's win in Super Bowl IV in 1970.

"We'd love to have that," Reid said. "At the same time, we have to go through the process and focus. We're playing a good football team. We need to go back and make a solid game plan and then come out and play well. That's really what it is, then good things happen." ▪

Opposite: Patrick Mahomes throws under pressure from Texans defensive end Charles Omenihu. Above: Travis Kelce dives for the endzone past cornerback Lonnie Johnson Jr.

AFC Championship

Chiefs 35, Titans 24
January 19, 2020 • Kansas City, Missouri

Red-Emption at Last

After 50 Years of Waiting, Chiefs Punch Ticket Back to Super Bowl

Shortly after watching the Denver Broncos top the Carolina Panthers in Super Bowl 50, Norma Hunt pulled aside her son Clark.

Clark's mother Norma is the widow of Lamar Hunt. Her late husband helped cajole seven other investors – the "Foolish Club" as they were known – to form the American Football League in 1960. It was Lamar who founded the Chiefs and helped facilitate the first AFL-NFL Championship game, eventually renamed Super Bowl I, a contest which his franchise lost to the Green Bay Packers in 1967.

Norma Hunt was at that game and every Super Bowl since. She's believed to the be only woman to attend every Super Bowl. She had something on her mind she wanted to tell her son.

"She said, 'Clark it sure would be nice if we could play in this game once while I'm still able to go,'" he said.

A full half century after Norma Hunt last watched her family's football team play in the Super Bowl, she saw her wish granted.

It wasn't easy. Just as the Houston Texans jumped on top of Kansas City in the Divisional playoff game a week earlier, the Tennessee Titans staked a 10-0 lead in the first quarter and led 17-7 with a little more than 6 minutes remaining before halftime.

Patrick Mahomes then put his MVP prowess on full display in the final minutes of the first half. When the Chiefs have fallen behind in the preseason, the team put its faith in the quarterback, Reid said.

"We all do, we all believe in him," Reid said. "It's not just me, it's everybody."

Mahomes punctuated his claim as the league's best player with a stellar performance over the final 40 minutes of the game. Mahomes completed 23-of-35 passing for three scores but it was "The Run" that added another clip to his career highlight reel.

The Chiefs lined up for a second-and-10 at the Titans 27-yard line with 23 seconds remaining in the first half. Mahomes took the snap and scanned for a receiver, but the Titans dropped seven defenders back in coverage, including double teams on Tyreek Hill and Travis Kelce.

The Chiefs' offensive line easily handled the three-man pass rush. Mahomes saw room to his left and took off with linebacker Rashaan Evans playing spy in pursuit. Mahomes momentarily slowed down, causing Evans to lose his pursuit angle. The quarterback ran through an arm tackle and found himself running free down the sideline.

"I was thinking about running out of bounds but as I got to the sideline, I realized I could cut up and I was running down the sideline and I knew we had two timeouts so I was like I might as well cut it back," Mahomes said.

Cornerback Tremaine Brock attempted to make a tackle but Mahomes spun away and propelled himself into the end zone with defensive tackle DaQuan Jones

Patrick Mahomes holds up the Lamar Hunt Trophy after the Chiefs secured their place in Super Bowl LIV.

landing on top of him. The touchdown put Kansas City up 21-17 at halftime, and they never looked back.

That play proved huge, Reid said.

"For him to be able to see that in the heat of it is something," Reid said. "He's got great eyes, great vision, which we know in the passing game, but he sees the whole picture and then he's able to find spots."

The resurgent Kansas City defense asserted itself in the second half, especially holding down running back Derrick Henry. The Titans rusher piled up 377 yards through his team's first two playoff games but the Chiefs held him to 69 yards on 19 carries, including just 7 yards in the second half.

The Chiefs hid their battle plan against Henry in plain sight. All week long defenders preached the need to hit him low and gang tackle, as linebacker Anthony Hitchens explained.

"The second time I had a chance to hit him low, I actually missed him," Hitchens said. "Then I went to the sideline and told my guys, 'Just because I missed him, it doesn't mean I'm going to stop going low.' That's the only way that you are going to get this guy down."

Tyrann Mathieu agreed that the defensive game plan against Henry was that simple.

"I don't think it was anything extra we needed to do defensively," Mathieu said. "It's just moreso about doing your job, understanding that one of us is going to have to make the tackle and the rest of us just have to rally to the ball. I thought we did a good job of that for the most part in the run game."

Kansas City rolled away with a 35-24 victory that didn't seem that close at the end, and Clark Hunt hoisted the trophy that bears his father's name in front of more than 73,000 cheering fans.

"It's a tremendous day for our family," Clark Hunt said. "I should mention how happy I am for my mother. For her to have the chance to hold and kiss this trophy, really means a lot."

Patrick Mahomes, Tyrann Mathieu and Travis Kelce celebrate their AFC Championship title.

The Chiefs last made the trip to the Super Bowl in January 1970. Clark Hunt, all of four years of age, attended the game with his family.

"I was at that game and I have a photo, so I hate to say that I don't really remember it," he said.

The Chiefs won three AFL championships, played in Super Bowl I and won Super Bowl IV during the franchise's first decade. It seemed unimaginable the team would go 22 years before winning another playoff game. The Chiefs made it to just one conference championship between 1970 and 2012, falling to Buffalo 30-13 in the AFC Championship in January 1994.

"It would not be what it is without the hardship, without all of the hard work that went into getting us here," Clark Hunt said. "Fifty years is too long, but we are going to Miami." ■

Above: Defensive end Frank Clark prepares to sack Titans quarterback Ryan Tannehill. Opposite: Patrick Mahomes runs for a touchdown against defensive tackle DaQuan Jones.